A CAVING MANUAL

A CAVING MANUAL

JIM LOVELOCK

B.T. BATSFORD, LONDON

First published 1981
© Jim Lovelock 1981

ISBN 0 7134 1904 0

Filmset in Monophoto Plantin by
Servis Filmsetting Ltd, Manchester

Printed in Great Britain by
The Anchor Press Ltd
Tiptree, Essex

for the publishers B.T. Batsford Ltd,
4 Fitzhardinge Street, London W1H 0AH

CONTENTS

ACKNOWLEDGMENTS

My thanks are due to many people who have assisted in the completion of this book and who have provided material, photographs and comment.

Among those I must mention are David Allsop of the Derbyshire Cave Rescue Organisation, and warden of Poole's Cavern, Buxton; Phil Brown, the equipment specialist of Caving Supplies, Buxton; Stanley Gee and Arthur Ball of the Derbyshire Caving Club and Peakland Archaeological Society; Bruce L. Bedford who has kept the light of *Descent* magazine shining through many difficult years; Alan L. Jeffreys and Ivan Young, for their invaluable help on the Scottish caving scene; Tony Oldham and his wife Anne, caving book sellers *extraordinaire* of Rhychydwr, Crymych, Dyfed; Denny Moorhouse of Clogwyn Climbing Gear, north Wales; M.K. (Ben) Lyon of Whernside Manor Cave and Fell Centre, Sedbergh; Sam Heath of Clam Products, Yorkshire; Tony Howard of Troll Safety Products, Oldham; Neil Montgomery, the Australian SRT specialist; Sheena Stoddard, probably Britain's best woman cave photographer; Peter Jackson and his father whose mining knowledge is second to none, especially in the Alston area; Dick Newell, President of Blue Water ropes, Florida; Peter Thompson of *Caving International Magazine*; and Jonathan Woods of Stockport Sub-Aqua Club. Other manufacturers have also weighed in, such as Oldham Batteries – and if anyone has been omitted, please forgive me.

Finally, I was in the closing stages of the production of this book when I received the tragic news that another friend had died in a cave diving accident. Ian Plant drowned whilst diving in Bull Pot near Barbon in March 1980. He had given me considerable help and encouragement in various matters of diving. As a fellow journalist, he was the highly regarded editor of the *Craven Herald*. I knew him from his Bury *Times* days and I know how delighted he was to obtain a senior post, at quite a young age, in the heart of his beloved caving country. This, then, is also a dedication to a superb caver, a fine journalist and a gentle, cultured man in all respects.

1
OF CAVES AND CURIOSITY

Lying on my back in a cave in Derbyshire, resting and looking at the roof I saw that it was made of scores of fossilised shells – a kind of oyster known as *producta gigantea*. It was, in fact, part of a sea bed. A few years later, in another, smaller cave near Everest, I came across something very like it again. Both events were a reminder that the centre of Britain – now equidistant from two oceans – and the highest mountain mass in the world, once formed part of a sea bed. This is only one example of the strange discoveries of exploring caves and potholes in the science known as speleology.

Alas, the public image of this fascinating pastime has been based, more often than not, on the unfortunate focus of the media on some dramatic rescue story or gruesome disaster. The inevitable comments at such times are 'Why do you do it?' – or 'It ought to be stopped because it risks lives and wastes public time and money'. This book will try to give an answer to the first question, as well as how to do it. As to the second comment – the simple answer is that it cannot be stopped and never will be while people have a healthy curiosity about our planet, its evolution and the life which has lived upon it.

The caves and potholes to which I shall be referring are in limestone, although there are other caves formed by different processes in lava, in sea cliffs and other rocks. I will also be referring to some mines and the miners, who, in pursuit of lead, were probably the first true explorers of the limestone regions. Limestone is almost wholly organic, formed from huge deposits of shells from molluscs such as *producta gigantea* and the remains of corals whose skeletons are composed of calcium carbonate drawn from the sea. These form the main ingredients of this curious grey-white rock. Through millions of years, the great impacted sea beds of this fossil-based rock have been thrown up in great geological upheavals which have shaped and re-shaped the Earth and which now stand high (but not always dry), sometimes thousands of yards thick, in many parts of the world. This is the raw material of the caver's underworld.

Nature has used two main tools to sculpt out complex

1   **The beautiful formations of the underworld, here in Column Hall, Ogof Ffynnon Ddu, south Wales.** *Sheena Stoddard*

9

subterranean systems – one is chemical, the other, force. Rainwater, picking up weak solutions of carbonic acid from the atmosphere and further concentrations from the soil and plant life, especially in peaty areas like the Peak District and Yorkshire, dissolves the apparently solid rock. The acidic erosion first attacks the weakest points, creating narrow cracks which, through aeons, gradually widen. As the water flow increases, its tremendous force, plus the carbonic acid, gouges away passages. Streams, rivers and waterfalls are part of the underground scenery. Seepage into the interstices of the rock may enlarge caverns by causing immense collapses as huge areas weaken and fall. An occasional shake in the Earth's crust helps to nudge the underworld into new shapes too. And whilst nature's tools are at work in this way, she is also going gently about the business of adorning this world of

2   The forest of stalagmites in the Hall of the Thirteen, Gouffre Berger, France, which dwarfs the human scale into insignificance. *Tony Briggs*

unending darkness with formations of strange and fascinating shape – stalactites, stalagmites, helictites, curtains, flowstone, rimstone pools or gours and stones like pearls or glittering crystals. Some are so fragile and delicate, such as the so-called straw stalactites, that they tremble at a breath. Some stalagmites are so big that they dwarf the human scale into insignificance. To these are added a wide variety of colours – the palette being the chemicals which the water acquires as it descends through the soil and other stratas creating scenes vibrant with colour.

From the earliest times caves have excited Man's wonder and awe and created the earliest myths and legends. Caves provided men with their first primitive homes and folklore. Apart from some animals which used caves as lairs, caves were the haunt of demons, dragons, gods and oracles. Goblins, dwarfs, giants, strange monsters, trolls and fairies are all supposed to have had their abodes underground. Bandits and holy

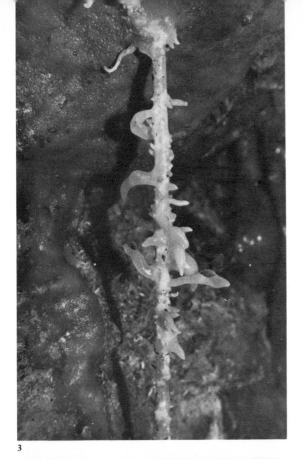

3

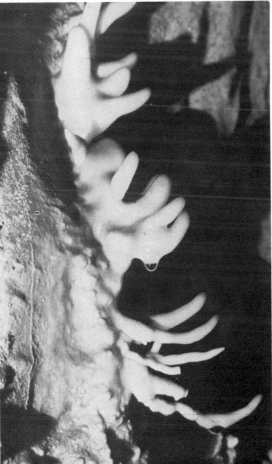

4

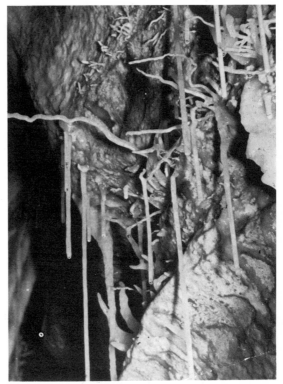

5

3–5   **Examples of strange helictite growth in south Wales: 3 & 4 in Ogof Ffynnon Ddu, the latter showing the famous 'Fingers' which are now severely damaged, and 5 in Pant Mawr.** *News Chronicle, Manchester*

men have also found caves convenient hide-aways; and, alas, today some caves are being used as dumping grounds for nuclear waste.

Before men developed the skills of home building, they lived like the animals in the cave entrances, convenient shelters from the elements and marauders. They did not, at first, penetrate very far, but they left evidence as to how they lived in the form of cooking utensils, ornaments and other signs of their growing domesticity. And they also left behind paintings and etchings on the rock which represent Man's earliest artistic endeavours. As David Attenborough has pointed out in his enthralling television series and its associated book, *Life on Earth*, one of the main distinctions between men and animals is that primitive Man was the first creature to paint representational pictures. Those found in Europe are the first known signs of Man's deeper penetration of his cavern abodes to create paintings which are remarkable by any standards.

I have been privileged to explore the famous caves at Lascaux in the Dordogne region of France, beyond the limits allowed to tourists, and have marvelled at the artistry of Cro-Magnon (or Stone Age) Man. I had the pleasure of exploring Lascaux with one of the original schoolboys who first discovered this treasury of primitive art in 1940. His dog disappeared into a hole which had previously been revealed by the uprooting of a tree during a storm. In seeking the dog, the boys ventured down a slope and their meagre lights revealed for the first time for possibly 15,000–20,000 years, this art of prehistoric Man.

Alas, modern Man, who exploited this remarkable monument as a show cave, was also responsible for the fungal invasion and erosion which threatened to destroy this art gallery of our forefathers. The exhalation of breath by hundreds of thousands of tourists and the incursion of algae from outside led to the closure of this world-famous cave. The battle to preserve the representations – once pristine, of bulls, buffaloes, horses, ibex – many including mysterious chevrons or arrows possibly associated with hunting rites, continues. Beyond the tourist limit, I was able to inspect one of the other curiosities, possibly the first representation of a bird in cave art. Meanwhile, as if to atone for this destruction, there has been in the past few years an immense and imaginative project to create an exact replica, correct to the finest detail and wrinkle in the rock, in the neighbouring hillside. In the nearby Les Combarelles cave at Les Eyzies, I have seen another example of primitive art, the engraved friezes produced, most likely, with a bone stylus or a sharp flint.

There is also something quite weird about the handprints in the Gargas cave in the Haute Garonne, each with some of the phalanges, parts of fingers and thumbs, missing. These handprints, some 200 or so, are believed to have had some religious or ritualist significance. One theory is that the missing parts may have been due to a primitive form of leprosy but the more general theory is that the joints were deliberately amputated in some strange rite. This poses a still unsolved ethnical problem for there are tribes in Central Africa and aborigines in Australia who still practise this form of hand mutilation. There are also some who create stencil paintings on the rock by blowing paint over their hands, possibly survivals from basic cultures which flourished before the continents drifted apart.

These are but a few of the examples of how caves had added more and more pieces to the jigsaw puzzle of evolution. Apart from primitive art, caves have yielded fragments which relate to the general picture of Man's progress all over the world. One of the most significant of these was the discovery of skeletal remains of one of our ancestors now thought to be 100,000 years old. The remains were recognised as important in 1856 by Dr Fuhlrott, a grammar school teacher, after workmen had blown open a cave in the Neander Valley near Dusseldorf during limestone quarrying. The bones, now known as Neanderthal Man (*Homo neanderthalensis*) revealed considerable brain development and were at first thought to be the possible missing link in the evolutionary gap between the apes and upright

men. Another fascinating find was in a cave at Dragon Bone Hill at Choukoutien, in Peking, and now known as Peking Man from a period nearly half a million years ago.

Britain has produced nothing as dramatic as this in the way of cave paintings or drawings (except, perhaps, the graffiti of cavers, miners and visiting tourists), or bones of such great antiquity. But I have taken part in diggings which have produced bones of some of our own island ancestors as well as the bones of animals long extinct in Britain, creatures which once roamed our hills before the great climatic changes drove them south seeking warmer parts. Some were probably left behind and died after the Channel 'bridge' subsided – strange to think of the hippopotamus, woolly rhinoceros, leopard, lion and grizzly bear living in Derbyshire – but there is ample evidence of their presence as well as of many others.

Apart from creatures long dead, the underworld sustains a number of life forms which, for some speleologists, become specialist studies in themselves. Bats are cave dwellers in many parts of the world and there are several bat colonies in Britain representing half a dozen varieties, the Greater and Lesser Horseshoe, the Long-eared, Daubenton's, the Whiskered and Natterer's. Studies of these creatures and their ability to navigate in total darkness have taken place over the centuries. Here, as elsewhere, bats have been ringed for study of their flight patterns and other habits. It was only in recent times that it was shown they have a sonar system, that is, high-frequency sound used for navigational purposes. I have stood in complete darkness in the flight path of bats leaving a cave, and although the bats were flying in a huge mass, not one

6 Apart from skulls like this, the bones of wild and domestic animals were found in Dowel Hall Cave, Derbyshire, as well as flints and domestic utensils.
Arthur Ball

7 **What a cave would look like without the lid! Gordale Scar in Yorkshire.**

crashed into me and all I felt was the gentle flutter of tiny wings as they zoomed away in pursuit of food. Bats, like homing pigeons, can navigate over hundreds of miles when taken from their home caves and released in strange territory.

Many people have an instinctive revulsion at the thought of bats, based, no doubt on the fearful folklore stories about vampires and films about Count Dracula. Bram Stoker has a lot to answer for! There *are* vampire bats of course, though not in this country and they get their blood supply only from animals. Perhaps the biggest danger to cavers from contact with these creatures is rabies, although I cannot find any reference to it in this country from a bat source. In any event, it is wise to wear gloves when handling bats for

8 & 9 Eyeless fish and crayfish live their entire life in total darkness. These are found in the underground streams of Mammoth Cave National Park. *National Park Service of the US Department of the Interior*

The fauna and flora of caves is fairly well divided into three types: trogloxenes, the occasional and often accidental visitors (show cave tourists probably come under this heading); troglophiles, species which choose caves for a habitat and flourish there; and troglobites whose life cycle is entirely in the world of darkness, species from the outside world entirely adapted and modified for continuous cave dwelling. Some of these latter have been called living fossils because they represent forms which have ceased to exist outside.

Because there is no sunlight or any other form of white light to affect pigmentation, such creatures that exist underground all the time are often of an albinoid appearance, a peculiar white colour. Fish develop without eyes as do other creatures which do not need them in the darkness. But while colour does not normally exist in permanent cave dwellers, I once had a strange experience in a French cave. Some distance inside we came across what looked like an immense spider with a domed, shell-like back which was a vivid red. Treating it as possibly poisonous we crawled gingerly under it – it was upside down on the roof of a fairly low crawl – promising to study it more closely on the return trip. When we came back, it had disappeared. None of my more scientific friends has been able to identify it and have made unkind references to over-indulgence in a Montignac bistro during the previous night's feast.

Beetles, spiders, centipedes, worms, shrimps are all subjects for the bio-speleologist. Britain has no salamanders, but these do inhabit caves in other parts of the world where the caves tend to be warmer. The salamander, in its cave form, was probably the first subterranean dweller to be noted by the scientist Von Valvasour in 1689. I have seen this strange creature in the caves of Postojna in Slovenia. Its scientific description is *Proteus anguinus* because of its snake-like appearance, but it is more commonly called the human fish because its colouration is like that of a white human. One of my Yugoslav caving friends told me that the cave salamander has the unusual ability to produce its young in two different ways: alive like tadpoles if the water is warm enough, or as eggs for subsequent hatching if the temperature is too cold.

Because of the absence of light, the flora of caves is also specially adapted to its environment and changes dramatically away from the cave entrance where some plants absorb enough light to obtain nutrition by photosynthesis. Further inside there are some fungi and algae and micro-organisms which are the field of the bacteriologist. In some caving regions of the world these studies are done on a fully scientific basis with specialised cave laboratories established.

ringing and other purposes, such as photography and measuring. In this connection, I would like to re-echo the plea of bat experts to cavers not to disturb the known colonies, as bats tend to leave home for good if their dwellings are invaded too frequently.

2
EARLY
EXPLORATIONS

Inevitably, Man's curiosity and the gradual advance of science, led him further and further into the Earth's caves and to speculate on his creation and what inhabitants, if any, it had. Professors or dilettante noblemen seeking knowledge or sensation overcame their fears of the unknown to venture into the impenetrable darkness. But it was not really until the

10 Caving garb, old style, with the superb 'Yorkshire' rope ladder at Rowten Pot, Kingsdale, Yorkshire. *F.H. Brindley*

nineteenth century that a truly scientific investigation began, mostly in horizontal directions. The great chasms, where they were known, were left alone. Cavers today acknowledge with respect those intrepid early explorers. It is remarkable to think that the first depth record ever achieved was in the Grotta di Trebiciano in the Carso Triestine in 1841 when an Italian team first descended over 1000 feet (305 metres) and reached a depth of 1086 feet (331 metres). This record stood until August 1925, when members of the Societa Alpina Giulie established a new world record of 1485 feet (453 metres) in the Raspo Abyss, near Pinguente.

One of the earliest attempts in Britain to establish the depth of one of the better known potholes occurred in the seventeenth century when Charles Cotton, the poetic friend of the great angler Izaak Walton, went along to Eldon Hole in Derbyshire, one of the Seven Wonders of the Peak District, and tried to work out how deep it was by throwing down a rope. Before that, the naturalist Charles Leigh decided Eldon Hole had been created by Noah's flood. In Elizabeth I's reign, Robert Dudley bribed a serf with gold to allow himself to be lowered down the hole. The historian Thomas Hobbes records the depth as 200 'ells' – around 750 feet (228 metres). The serf returned unconscious, his hair had gone white and he died soon afterwards, apparently from shock. Eldon Hole was my first pothole, and after my first descent, I know exactly how that serf felt.

Cotton's experiment with a line must have been conducted with a certain amount of poetic licence as he made the depth of Eldon just over half a mile – 2652 feet (808 metres). The experience inspired him to write a long poem in which he wrote

. . . who dare
Look down into the Chasme, and keep his Hair
From lifting off his Hat, either has none,
Or for more Modish Curls, casheers his own.

He perpetuated some of the legends about Eldon including the one about the goose which fell down the hole and eventually emerged at Peak Cavern at Castleton with all its feathers burnt off, having presumably passed through the fires of Hell. Apart from the bit about passing through the fires of Hell, this legend may have been based on fact, because there is a school of thought among cave explorers in Derbyshire who believe that there might well be a link between Eldon and the great show cave of Peak Cavern. The first actual descent of Eldon was made in 1777 by Mr John Lloyd, FRS, who got to the bottom and recorded in *Philosophical Transactions* that the depth was exactly 186 feet (57 metres). He prosaically recorded that: 'The light, however, which came from above, was sufficient for the reading of any print.' He survived the bombardment of falling stones as he was brought out to give what was probably the first recorded description of the descent of a pothole.

With a few exceptions, the early investigations of caves were in pursuit of the bones of early men and animals. Excavations were limited to cave entrances; only occasionally did anyone delve any deeper than the limits of natural light. Lack of knowledge and imperfect equipment restricted the earliest explorations. But stemming from the search for bones and signs of prehistory there developed a curiosity in the form and structure, the very causes of caves and their associated shafts which are now called potholes. Geologists and paleontologists developed a mutual interest in how nature had created its hidden wonderland. They speculated on the source of rivers which suddenly disappeared underground or emerged from the foot of some cliff. It was natural for this growing interest to evolve into a science itself. The need to get down the shafts, to travel long distances in a world of unending darkness, to follow the underground water passages and lakes and to counter the difficulties and dangers led inevitably to the evolution of the specialised techniques necessary for this form of exploration. Present-day mountaineering evolved in somewhat similar fashion. The first mountains were climbed for scientific or philosophical reasons. The brothers Jean-André and Guillaume-Antoine Deluc of Geneva went to the top of the Buet to experiment with air pressure at altitude and also to test the boiling point of water above sea level. De Saussure first went to Mont Blanc as a naturalist. The Abbé Murith climbed the Velan because, as a botanist, he wanted to find out how high plants grew on the mountains. It was only later that mountaineering became an end in itself. So it was with cave exploration, now known as speleology.

The father of modern speleology was the intrepid Frenchman Edouard-Alfred Martel, who pioneered many techniques which are still in use today. Almost certainly it was his visit to Britain before the turn of the century which gave the impetus to the caving movement over here. In fact speleology may have started in Britain out of sheer pique that a Frenchman should lead the way to the bottom of one of the country's biggest potholes. For many years Gaping Gill had had the same fascination for Yorkshiremen that Eldon Hole had for men in the High Peak of Derbyshire. It did not have the same wealth of folklore and legend but the prospect of descending this massive hole in the limestone enticed many to make the attempt.

Nowadays there are two well-known entrances to the Gaping Gill system. One is Bar Pot, an insignificant little opening at the foot of a small limestone cliff which was not discovered or descended until September 1949. The other is the main shaft on the east side of Ingleborough which is one of the wonders of the shire of the broad acres.

11 **Bar Pot entrance to the Gaping Gill system.** *News Chronicle, Manchester*

The Fell Beck, chattering merrily over its stony bed, suddenly plunges into the mouth of a wide fissure in the limestone and hurtles down dramatically until its white spume is lost in the greater darkness. It is an impressive sight. It is even more impressive when one climbs down a swaying ladder or plunges down crazily on a bosun's chair attached to a winch cable. Possibly the first recorded attempt to descend 'GG', as it is affectionately known in caving circles, was that of John Birbeck of Settle in the heart of the caving country. He tried in 1872. Realising the hazard from the powerful flow of water into the pothole he set about diverting the Fell Beck. With help, he dug a trench nearly 1000 yards (914 metres) long along which he diverted the waters of the stream. This done, he managed to lifeline the main shaft and succeeded in descending to a ledge about 200 feet (61 metres) down, a remarkable achievement in those days. He had to be pulled out.

In the summer of 1895, Martel came over from Paris on a tour of the known caves and potholes of Britain and Ireland. It was the year of the formation of the first speleological club in France where the sport-cum-science had already taken a firm hold. By then, Martel had already evolved the use of rope ladders and a system of lifelining borrowed, most likely, from the early rope technique of Alpine climbers. Edward Whymper had been one of the first to write about the art of rope management and its correct use on steep rocks and on ice. Martel was also probably the first man to recognise the value of the telephone to cave explorers. One of the problems of speleology is that of communication between members of a caving party who may be separated on the various pitches of a pothole or extended through the length of a cave. In some places it is possible to use a code of whistle signals but highly efficient field telephones and occasionally radio links are more reliable and practical. Martel used a telephone in Gaping Gill. It was a primitive affair and was subject to rather more malfunctioning than is the present-day instrument.

Martel made his historic descent on 1 August 1895 and, as this marked what might be called the birth of speleology in Britain, it is worth recording fairly fully. The news of his attempted descent brought a sizeable crowd over the moors to the pothole entrance and they watched with interest as he tied his long lengths of ladder together, measured out what he felt was sufficient safety line and, through his English-speaking wife, gave his helpers instructions on the management of the rope. He had tried several days before but the English summer was as unpredictable as ever and thunderstorms swelled the beck to alarming proportions. By noon on 1 August, however, conditions had improved sufficiently for him to make the attempt.

There was no shortage of willing hands to hold the lifeline, in fact there were so many as to represent a positive danger. With the air of a man who knew exactly what he was doing, Martel raised his cap, adjusted his lantern and stepped over the edge on to his ladder. As he made his slow descent, Mme Martel relayed his instructions to the lifeline party as they came crackling over the wires. Like a true explorer, Martel was duly cautious. He left little to chance and he paused frequently to evaluate his position. Daylight gradually faded as his practised feet sought out the rungs beneath him. He was immensely strong and possessed extraordinary stamina. This he needed when he first climbed into the waterfall. Although the Fell Beck had been diverted somewhat, it was not possible then, as it is today, wholly to prevent the stream from cascading down the shaft. There was a

considerable body of water thundering down what is described as England's highest single-drop waterfall, as Martel was hit by its full force. Although anticipating it, his breath was taken away for a few minutes. I know only too well how he felt, as I have been stuck in the same waterfall myself. Even with present-day waterproof equipment, it is always an unpleasant experience. How long one stays in the wet depends on the sense of humour of the man driving the winch.

12 (Left) Gaping Gill and (right) Edouard-Alfred Martel on his famous descent in 1895.

Around 190 feet (58 metres) from the surface, Martel touched down on the same ledge which Birbeck found twenty-three years previously. Here, he stopped while he carefully sorted out the coils of rope ladder and safety line which had piled up on the ledge. Although it looks and sounds quite easy, it is often difficult to throw a ladder correctly down the full length of a deep pitch of a pothole. It can snag and snarl on all kinds of projections on land or ledges far from the bottom. Leaning out from the ledge with the lifeline taking the strain, Martel was able to guide the ladder down the remainder of the shaft. But his light was feeble and the daylight from above was too poor to show whether or not it had actually reached the bottom. He had taken careful soundings previously and was satisfied that he had sufficient ladder for his task. But he was still uncertain. He paused to look up at the waterfall spurting just beyond him. In some lighting conditions it gives off a lovely rainbow effect, but overhead it was a dull day and his lamp, by modern standards, was a bare glimmer. The fall was deafening and ominous but Martel stepped boldly from his ledge having assured his helpers, over the telephone, that all was well and he seemed certain of reaching the bottom safely. As he descended further, the ladder began to sway alarmingly just below where the roof of the main cave abuts on to the wall of the main shaft. This motion carried Martel in and out of the waterfall, ducking him repeatedly.

The force of the water knocked him breathless. To add to his difficulties, Martel realised he had miscalculated the length of his safety line and he reached the end of it before getting to the bottom of the cave. Over the telephone, he called to his helpers to tie on another length. The roar of the water rushing past him made it impossible to tell whether his message had been heard and understood. He dangled, drenched to the skin, clinging in the icy blackness to the rope ladder. As the rope round his waist slackened, he sensed that a new length of line had been added and he set off down the last few feet to the cave floor. To the watchers above, and no doubt to Martel himself, it seemed like an age between leaving the edge of the pothole and reporting his safe arrival at the bottom. It took, in fact, twenty-three minutes.

Calmly, over the telephone he announced: 'I have reached the bottom. I will untie myself and go and explore the cave.' Before he did so, with true Gallic appreciation of the needs of the inner man, he told his helpers, 'You can now have lunch.' While the surface party were eating their sandwiches and wondering if they would ever see Martel again, the Frenchman was placidly perambulating round the Main Chamber, which covers over half an acre and is more than 100 feet (30 metres) high. It must have been an awe-inspiring sight for him to look upwards. The waterfall thudded on to a pile of rocks, some of which had fallen from the shaft sides and others which had been lobbed in by passers-by. From top to bottom, the shaft is 350 feet (107 metres) deep and the waterfall is one of the most dramatic sights in British caving. By the faint light of his lantern, Martel probed around the Main Chamber, which is 500 feet (152 metres) long, noting the various passages leading away from this ante-room of the underworld. He surmised, quite rightly, that this was only the beginning of a big cave system. As later explorations proved, it is one of the biggest systems in Britain, extending for nearly 4 miles (6½ kilometres) with at least one other entrance in addition to Bar Pot, the extremely severe Car Pot with its immensely narrow and difficult link into the East Passage of Gaping Gill.

Writing later, Martel commented: 'It was one of the most amazing subterranean scenes I have ever witnessed.' As he had already been in some of the greatest gulfs in France, this was tribute indeed to the splendours of the Yorkshire underworld. In spite of his limited equipment and poor lighting, Martel was able to make a quick preliminary survey and a reasonably accurate sketch of what he had seen. This done, his chattering teeth warned him that cold and fatigue, among the worst enemies of cavers, were setting in. Although it was summer, the cave was far from warm – no caves ever are.

He returned to his telephone, which he had tucked under a rock for safety. Eagerly he called the surface. 'Allô! Allô! Allô!' he shouted into the instrument. 'Tirez doucement. . . . Entendez-vous?' There was no answer from those above. The line was dead. Water must have made its insidious way into the primitive handset and shorted the connections. Or the line may have been snicked by a rock. Whatever the reason, he was out of vocal contact with his helpers. But he had also arranged a few signals which were to be given on the safety line in the event of the telephone breaking down. Wisely, he tied himself on first, before giving the first tugs to let those above know he was ready to come out. I say 'wisely' because potholers who have failed to tie on before giving rope signals have found the loose end whisked out of their hands and it is not always easy to get the rope down to exactly the right spot again. No sooner had his signals been understood than the belay party started hauling away with immense enthusiasm and vigour. So much so that poor Martel's feet hardly touched the rungs, and he was jerked skywards like a pantomime fairy in an aerial ballet. Just as suddenly the pulling stopped. The rope had probably jammed in a crevice or become wedged between the ladder and the rock. It was certainly not a healthy place for that to happen and Martel was left to admire the scenery while the belay party tugged and tugged to free the line. To help them, Martel climbed a few rungs to give the rope some slack and this was sufficient to unwedge the rope and allow the pulling to continue unhampered. He paused for a rest on the ledge and then made the rest of the ascent without incident. At exactly 3.55 p.m. he was back at the entrance to the shaft and the muggy warmth which greets potholers on their return from the cold realms below. He bowed modestly to the cheering crowd and politely avoided the pats on the back which might have knocked him down the shaft again at a faster rate than he had recently descended it. It was an emotional occasion. His wife kissed him passionately. A hot rum was quickly provided. Dry clothes were donned. Martel was once again the immaculate Frenchman. And courteous as always. He never forgot the assistance given to him by many Yorkshire folk, whose chagrin at seeing their greatest chasm fall to a foreigner he must have sensed. He was truly grateful and, when writing of the conquest of Gaping Gill, he commented: 'My Gaping Gill public was the calmest and most sensible I ever came across.'

13 The author (right) helping Geoffrey Workman return up Bar Pot after his first stay down of 14 days alone in Gaping Gill. *News Chronicle, Manchester*

Martel's feat echoed throughout Britain. It was a gauntlet thrown down to Yorkshiremen on their native heath and the challenge was not slow in being accepted. The doughty Yorkshire Ramblers' Club, formed in that golden age when men were first turning to their native hills for mental and physical recreation and escape from industrial squalor, tackled the hole a few years later. They used a winch instead of a ladder and started the series of explorations which have now uncovered most of the secrets of this truly remarkable cave.

Perhaps it was not without significance that the weather should shed a few tears on Martel after he made his descent. Only twenty minutes after his return to the surface a violent storm broke over Ingleborough, swelling the beck so much that, had Martel been on his ladder then, he could easily have been swept away. Today Gaping Gill is classified as a Super Severe pothole in the graduated standards of difficulty by which caves and potholes are known. I have been down there for five days on a big exploration. Geoffrey Workman established the first British staydown record in Gaping Gill when he remained alone for a fortnight, camping in the Sand Cavern and carrying out a great deal of research into the cave and also into human behaviour in isolation underground.

Speleology in Britain began with Martel. Ironically, it was a British team which beat the French at their own

game when they achieved the caving equivalent of climbing Everest, establishing a new world depth record in the Gouffre Berger, the deepest known cave in France, which was first descended by the French.

Since my first book, *Caving*, was first published, I have continually been taken to task for not giving sufficient mention of that doyen of Mendip cavers, Herbert Balch. He was inspired, when in his teens, by listening to a lecture given by the great Sir William Boyd Dawkins, on his excavations at Wookey Hole. Balch is one of the father figures of British speleology and one of the earliest to write of his experiences in a way which excited others to follow him into Wookey, Swildon's Hole, Eastwater Swallet and Lamb Lair (or Leer). The latter was discovered, as were so many other caves in the early days, by lead miners in 1670.

Balch was indefatigable in his work until his death in 1958 at the ripe old age of eighty-nine. He also has the doubtful distinction of being Britain's first potholing accident in Lamb Lair in the 60 foot (18 metres) pitch leading into the main chamber. Whilst leading a party of men and women, Balch was descending on a rope attached to an old windlass when the rope snapped and he plunged to the bottom. He had earlier enquired if the rope, which unknown to him had been stored under a leaky roof in a gamekeeper's shed, had been tested with a weight. It should have been done with an iron skep (skip or basket) filled with stones. But this

14   The main chamber of Lamb Lair Cavern, the Mendip Hills. It was discovered by lead miners in 1670. *Sheena Stoddard*

had not been done – and the inevitable happened. A reminder, perhaps, to be wary of taking the words of others when life depends upon the truth. I had a somewhat similar experience on the old winch in Nettle Pot in Derbyshire shortly after World War II. This time it was the winch which partially collapsed after I had been assured it was quite safe and firmly anchored. Luckily I suffered a drop of no more than a few feet and the painful intrusion of the rope into my rib cage. Balch lay unconscious for some time with his fingers cut to the bone from grasping another and thinner cotton line used down the shaft to stop people from spinning giddily on the winch rope. This probably saved his life because it enabled him to keep his head upright when he hit the ground. In those days there were no such things as helmets – he usually wore an old trilby hat. Rescue was soon at hand but his injuries long remained. It is an indication of the courage of the man who, following this accident, wrote: 'For a long time, I could not think of the experience without perspiration breaking out on hands

and face, reduced somewhat after the next trip down, which I forced myself to face.'

These, then, were some of the pioneers who laid down many of the first principles of cave exploration. The Yorkshire Ramblers' Club, the Kyndwr Club (the old spelling of Kinder Scout) in Derbyshire and the Wells Natural History Society in the Mendip Hill were the first organised bodies of speleologists. South Wales was a little slow off the mark in this respect although it has some of Britain's longest cave systems and the earliest work there was undertaken by individuals. There was no national organisation such as the Société Spéléologique de France founded by Martel himself until much later with the formation of the British Speleological Association, and later still, the British Cave Research Association.

Contrary to popular opinion, many cavers survive to respectable old age. Martel was seventy-seven when he died after a lifetime of exhausting exploration and the writing of hundreds of papers and books. Cave litera-

15　Excavating in caves reveals many mysteries. Here a skull is being unearthed in Dowel Hall Cave, Derbyshire, in a neolithic burial chamber. *Arthur Ball*

ture, in the modern sense, began with him and his works are classics of their kind. Another contributor to the growing volume of writing on caving was Ernest A. Baker, MA, whose book *Moors, Crags and Caves of the High Peak and Neighbourhood* published in 1903, stimulated the movement towards and under the hills. He was one of the first to conceive the idea of caving as a sport. In his description of his descent of Eldon Hole he observed: 'Rock climbing above ground is fascinating sport; to enjoy it below the surface and in semi-darkness, would be to catch a rarer thrill. . . .'

It became apparent that in caving there remained the one true form of exploration left in this country, to go where no-one had been before. All our mountains had been climbed, almost every inch of the surface surveyed – but far below the ground there was, and still is, the possibility of new discoveries with the thrill of treading where no human foot has gone before. Weekend after weekend and often daily throughout holiday times, digging, diving, blasting and sometimes

with sheer bare-handed labour, cavers are continually finding something new. Luck sometimes comes into it in finds which have existed close at hand for years. With the development of new equipment and techniques, the possibilities have increased enormously, as these enable the caver to spend more of his precious time underground. The writer William Bolitho once defined adventure as the 'practice of the art of the impossible'. In caving, as in climbing, the criteria of the impossible have changed dramatically, with each generation of cavers giving impetus to the next. Cavers have gained inspiration from men like Eric Hensler who made the solo discovery and traverse of the 1300 foot (400 metre) bedding plane in Gaping Gill – one of the longest and continuously tight crawls in Britain, if not the world. This was way back in 1937. Even by today's standards of toughness and fitness, it is still an extremely hard caving trip and the passage bears his name as a lasting memorial. Again, as if to prove that longevity in cavers is the rule, rather than the exception, this incredible man revisited the scenes of his former triumph in 1965 on his sixty-fifth birthday. The whole caving world in its international sense was saddened in August 1978 with the news of the death of Dr Edgar Tratman at the age of seventy-nine. A Bristolian, he is also numbered among those who helped to elevate caving from a mere pastime for a Sunday afternoon to an exacting science.

Linkages, through-trips, longer and longer sump dives have developed into regular features. Yorkshire, Derbyshire, the Mendip Hills, south Wales – even Scotland, have all yielded new secrets and some of the dreams of my youth have now become realities. With all this going on and the contribution of distinguished scientists such as Dr Anthony Waltham, British caving began to emerge from its hole-in-the-corner image and has gained a new respectability. Today, there are probably about 20,000 cavers in Britain and clubs now number hundreds where there were just a few. The club growth rate tends to reflect the individuality, odd though it may sound, of cavers and the splintering break-aways often for personal and other reasons. After many set-backs and doubts, Britain now has its own national caving associations, which have achieved the near impossible task of unifying the voice of caving. There are now national bodies for cave rescue, cave diving and the registry of caves. Caving instructors also have their own organisation. International links have been strengthened through the International Speleological Congress. Britain was host to the ISC conference in 1977, acclaimed as the most successful ever held.

The image of caving has changed dramatically and British cavers have had a growing record of achievements during recent years, not only in the conventional

16 This baulk of timber blocked part of the way in a Derbyshire dig. Where it came from and how it got there no one knows.

17 Award-winning BBC cameraman Syd Perou with his caving Bolex. *Daily Mirror*

caving areas of Europe but further afield in Arctic Norway, Iran, the Himalayas, New Guinea, Peru and Sarawak. Some of these expeditions have been on the large scale of comparable Himalayan ventures with financial support which, hitherto, was not forthcoming. The general public – whose interest in caves has been confined to show caves and stories of rescues, has had its appetite whetted by a number of films seen on television. The superb camera work of BBC cameraman Syd Perou has rightly won international acclaim. His series on the underground of Yorkshire proved to be gripping viewing as was the superb film made by producer Barry Cockcroft of Yorkshire TV, who, with his chief cameraman Mustofa Hammuri, made the thrilling account of the record-breaking dive at Keld Head by Oliver 'Bear' Statham and Geoff Yeadon.

One golden age of British caving has passed but there are signs that a new one is well on its way in Britain and elsewhere. One of the tragedies of the times is that many areas of potential exploration are in politically sensitive and strife-torn regions which may inhibit the sending of expeditions for some time. But there are new depths to conquer on Earth; and, it is quite within the bounds of possibility for there to be caves and potholes of various kinds on the planets. It has been suggested that the lunar explorers found no-one on the Moon because they were all living underground!

3
PERSONAL EQUIPMENT

In the days before cave exploration became as highly organised and scientific as it is now on an international basis, there was a fairly light-hearted and casual approach to sojourns underground. A few old clothes, nailed boots, a torch, a few candles, a length of hemp rope and wide-runged wooden ladders – and the inevitable flat cap – were adequate enough items of equipment for the pioneers of caving. In his book *La France Ignorée* – now beautifully reprinted by Lafitte Reprints of Marseille, E.-A. Martel is seen in what appears to be a dress suit, a trilby type hat and a candle on top. Other photographs of these fearless French pioneers show them in Panama hats and boaters. I also have a photograph of a dour-looking Mr E. Simpson, first secretary of the BSA, making a descent in Yorkshire nattily dressed in a trilby and an old mackintosh.

The attire of some early cavers appears to have been acquired from jumble sales and theatrical costumiers. Later, after World War II, cavers seized on ex-War Department left overs – overalls, old RAF survival kits, ammunition boxes, Commando karabiners which tended to open or pull straight, entrenching tools and dinghies – all adapted to caving use. Improvisation was the order of the day when I started my caving after the war. At that time the relatively small number of people caving did not warrant any commercially minded enthusiast producing purpose-made caving equipment. But as the sport boomed and began to appeal to growing numbers of adventure-minded people, mostly young, new thinking took place in attitudes to, and the use of, equipment. At first there were the inevitable spin-offs from the progress made in climbing which involved not only equipment, but the philosophy as well. Man-made fibres replaced the old hemp and manilla ropes, wire ladders with light-weight metal rungs replaced the cumbersome 'Yorkshire' and other rope and wood ladders and, with the closure of many old mines up and down the country, the miners' long-life rechargeable batteries became available as did their helmets. Then, so-called open-air equipment shops began to proliferate (I had one myself) and experts in mountaineering and caving began to turn their know-how into business and manufacturing enterprises. Blacks of Greenock were probably first in the field with the mass production of their light-weight wire ladder

18 Mr E. Simpson, first secretary of the BSA, on a Yorkshire descent, nattily dressed in trilby and mackintosh. *Frank H. Brindley*

19 Three typical caving helmets – the Petzl, the most expensive, in the middle.

which was the beginning of the end of those club nights spent patiently assembling do-it-yourself rope ladders (my club got its rung timber from a friendly undertaker, which was a constant reminder to make things good and true to avoid his professional services!). Manufacturers of mountaineering equipment turned their attention to the specialist needs of the caving world and the caver began to be catered for in his own right. Commercialism has now become an important issue. Purists regard this as regrettable but it has led to faster, safer and more ambitious caving trips and the achievement of new 'ultimates' in many parts of the world.

In this chapter on personal equipment, I will start at the top. The old caving joke was that people wore something on their heads only to prevent the cranium from damaging the rock, useful also to keep matches and cigarettes dry. My caving career began in Eldon Hole in Derbyshire with a balaclava helmet as a modicum of protection against falling rocks and later progressing to a 'battle bowler' from an ex-GI which was useful in preventing one's ears being ripped off in a tight cranny. Today the range of headgear includes adaptations of industrial safety helmets manufactured to appropriate British Standards Institute specifications, to what I call the Rolls Royce of helmets, that made by Etablissements Petzl of Grenoble. The Petzl helmet was created especially for caving with a mixed light facility – a battery headlamp system and an acetyline light with electric ignition as well. The price is around £33 and it now only remains for someone to put in a two-way radio, as has been demonstrated in a new climbing helmet, to take it into the £100 bracket. A helmet must be a good fit and must not wobble on the head. An ill-fitting helmet is likely to flop about and drop over the eyes as well as making disconcerting shifts of the light beam. To this end, an adequate chin strap should be a consideration, as should a rear fastening for cables or wires from batteries to headlamps. The trend is also towards the peakless climber's helmet such as the Petzl although a peak is useful in helping to provide a base for a carbide lamp in addition to the helmet clip.

As the caving scene is one of unending darkness – the blackness is absolute – portable, artificial lighting must be carried. The earliest explorers used candles and these are still a useful and dependable part of a caver's auxiliary or survival lighting equipment, providing he keeps his matches dry. The candles may also be eaten as a last resort. Much romantic and other nonsense has been written about candlelight. It was probably true when Emerson wrote that in pitch darkness the smallest candle fills a mile with its ray. The great Mendip man, Herbert Balch, regarded the candle as the most dependable light, its main virtue being that it cast no treacherous shadows which, as a piece of caver's doggerel points out, is due to it giving no 'bloody light'. My old friend Roland Revel of Bagshawe Cavern fame still swears by them, however. There are several long-life varieties.

Next comes the good old carbide lamp which has now reached a highly efficient form with reflectors of various sizes. Some cavers prefer carbide lamps to electric ones because, once they become familiar with their use, they find the lamps give a fairly large area of light, equally diffused and better to work by than some electric lights which give a powerful beam but create cones of darkness. The main advantages of carbide lamps are that if spare carbide and water are carried, they are rechargeable *in situ*, useful for warming the hands, heating drinks, or detecting the presence of heavy concentrations of carbon-dioxide which is present in some mines. They also have a number of disadvantages. Water will, of course, put them out, so they cannot be used for diving under 'ducks' or on waterfall pitches. They can be extinguished by strong draughts. Care must be exercised in the use of carbide lamps close to the body, especially near to the eyes and hair – or the backside of the person in front in a crawl. They should also be kept well away from any ropes of man-made fibres which melt under heat. In confined spaces, it is as well to switch from carbide lighting to electric, as burning acetyline tends to consume oxygen fairly rapidly and this may affect breathing. It must be remembered too that the gas itself, if allowed to escape in a confined space, can have unpleasant results. Acetyline may not be lethal but its presence can cut down the oxygen supply to below that of the body's minimum requirements. There is a suspicion that it will contain traces of phosphine –

phosphoretted hydrogen – which is, of course, both highly toxic and a fire hazard. I have no doubt that the carbide light he had on his helmet was one of the contributory factors in the death of a university student, Neil Moss, in Peak Cavern, Castleton, Derbyshire, in March 1959. After being on the superhuman rescue attempts to save his life, I attended the inquest at which a pathologist pointed out that the oxygen in the narrow tube in which Moss was trapped would be consumed by his acetyline light, replacing it with carbon dioxide. This led, inevitably to his death from anoxia (lack of oxygen) and his entombment for ever in the Derbyshire limestone.

As carbide needs water to activate it into a gas, water for this purpose must either be available underground or carried in a spare container. The carbide itself

20 (below) Glutinous muddy passage in Peak Cavern, Derbyshire, where French cavers helped in the unsuccessful attempt to free Neil Moss who died and remains interred there. *Paris-Match, Marie-Claire*

21 (right) Caver re-filling his carbide lamp with water, in Norway.

should not be too large – there is a British Standards Institute specification for it – and it should be carried in a completely sealed and watertight container. Ignition may be achieved electrically but, more usually, from a flint-wheel mounted in the reflector, or from another carbide lamp or naked flame. Cleanliness is the most important part of maintaining a carbide lamp which, with regular servicing and the availability of spare parts, should give many years of service. The lamp should be thoroughly cleaned after use, and the flint should be checked and changed, if necessary. Lastly, never, never, throw away your spent carbide in a cave and always pick up any which may be spilled when recharging the base of the lamp. The threat to a cave environment from such cast-off chemicals is obvious and is often considered to be the major criticism against the use of carbide lights in caves.

There is a wide variety of electric portable lighting suitable for caving, both wet and dry cell batteries. The choice of lighting is sometimes governed by the projected length of the trip underground. There are a number of headlamps on the market which operate from the U2 type of batteries or the oblong 'doorbell'

type which has two brass screw terminals and is a convenient size to fit into a breast pocket. The disadvantage of the 'doorbell' battery is that it tends to disintegrate when the cardboard container gets wet and it is a good idea to protect it with insulation tape or a plastic pouch. The headlights are usually attached by means of an elasticated band which tends to perish after a few wet caving trips. Some varieties, such as the French Achil Wonder Light and some of those manufactured by Pifco have plastic or metal battery cases which have attachments for fixing to waist belts. Reserve batteries have to be carried and these should be in sealed containers. As with spent carbide, discharged batteries should be brought out of the cave.

The lights most often used these days are the rechargeable variety which became available in large numbers as various mines closed down. Many of these were refurbished and made serviceable for cavers. There are two basic types – alkaline and lead acid. The former is little used nowadays because leaking alkali is capable of inflicting nasty burns, as some cavers know to their cost, although the batteries themselves have proved remarkably durable. I think it is fair to say that

British cavers invariably go for the Oldham lead-acid batteries used in conjunction with the same firm's Intersafe heavy duty helmet which conforms to the British Standards Institute specification 2826. Many good old lamps of Oldham manufacture are still available in a reconditioned state and, apart from the firm itself which is based in Denton, Manchester, the leading authority and suppliers are J.A. Jones (Mining) at Glossop in Derbyshire. At the time of writing, Oldham Batteries' latest battery and head set is the T type which has a lighter and tougher battery case than previous models, the weight being a little over 5 lb (2.3 kg). The topping up process has been improved by non-return holes, with no plugs to remove and a visible electrolyte level. This, and a similar type of battery, requires recharging with a special charger. Many cavers find it useful to invest in a single type charger in order to do their own charging appropriate to their own knowledge of the use the lamp has had and the number of hours it has been discharged. The single charger, however, is not automatic, ceasing when the lamp has taken its full charge. This is only possible in the multiple charging units which some clubs acquire for weekly charging sessions. As with all other caving equipment, lighting sets require regular and careful maintenance. Batteries should be topped up with distilled water only and care should be taken not to overfill them. Where an alkaline cell battery is still in use, all surplus electrolyte should be removed – a weak solution of vinegar is useful for this and any acid may be dealt with by an antacid such as sodium hydrogen carbonate in its common form of baking powder.

Cavers have also been turning their attention to the Vidor range of Sealed Lead Acid Batteries made by Crompton Parkinson of South Shields, which combine the characteristics of conventional lead-acid batteries in that they are rechargeable, with the greater safety factor and ease of handling of ordinary dry batteries. This range uses a gelled electrolyte which is completely sealed off so that there is no danger from spilled electrolyte, and also eliminates the risk of dangerous gas or spray emissions during the charging. Nor is there any need to check electrolyte levels or undertake the normal, regular topping up process, and they are available in 6 volt and 12 volt forms. But they do need a certain amount of adaption for caving use, such as changing the bulbs in the headlamp to accommodate the different output. Another problem is that of re-charging and Vidor recommend a constant charging system. This requires a certain amount of electrical knowledge if one wants to make such a system oneself, but suitable manufactured ones are available from Shorrock Security Systems of Blackburn, Lancashire.

These, then are the main lighting sources in use in caving. Additionally, hand torches, preferably the floatable, waterproof variety, are extremely useful for poking into crevices. On big trips, especially where photography is involved, a Tilley paraffin lamp or the large, hand-held acetyline lamps are also useful when weight and porterage present no problems. Before making a descent, all lighting gear should be checked. As I have stressed, maintenance is all important. I should also mention here, although it applies equally to chapter 8, Food, Survival and Emergency, lighting equipment could include the so-called 'lightsticks' or chemical lights developed originally for military use. These provide a light of greenish luminosity due to chemical reaction when the small, plastic tube is bent or broken and the constituent chemicals intermingle. In conditions of complete blackness, the light is adequate for making repairs to failed or damaged equipment or sufficient to negotiate one's way. The effective light lasts for up to about three hours although these have been known to keep on glimmering for much longer than that. These chemical lights may be carried either inside the helmet, in a supply tin or in a suitable pocket.

Now, clothing. This is another aspect of caving which has undergone significant changes in the past few years with various manufacturers turning their attention to the specialist needs of cavers. Some of the clothing are spin-offs from sub-aqua diving and water skiing where, as in caving, the need is to keep water out, preserve body temperature and prevent exposure (hypothermia). For the simplest form of trip in dry caves or mines where water is not a problem, a sensible garb will include woollen underwear or Long Johns, light sweaters and a one-piece overall boiler-suit. The underwear depends upon what your body can tolerate – some people cannot stand wool next to their skin, whereas I come out in a rash with nylon. I once had a talk with the late Wilson Hey, a member of my own climbing club, the Rucksack Club, and pioneer in the battle to have morphia included in mountain rescue kits. Discussing clothing and exposure, he gave me some good advice – 'Keep the viscera warm, lad. Keep the viscera warm,' he said patting my belly firmly. I have found this extremely sound advice and have often used woollen bathing trunks for this purpose.

Because of their insulating quality, string vests and string underpants are useful and are also valuable in absorbing sweat. The alternation between a lather of perspiration during extreme exertion, and the sudden cooling of the body due to immersion or waiting around, have always been a problem and the absorbtive quality of undergarments is a consideration in their choice. The one-piece boiler suit must be large enough to go over all the other clothing with ample room to fully raise the hand above the head and stretch and bend the legs. Too many pockets are a nuisance and anything in them tends to bunch and snarl on obstructions. There are a number of makes of thermal wear on the market which have evolved for high altitude climbing and polar expeditions, such as the suits with fur-pile linings which are exceedingly warm. Some of this wear is available as military surplus and is consequently cheaper.

22 A modern caver, using SRT, rappel rack, sit-harness, wellies and one-piece suit with reinforced knees. Taken in Papua, New Guinea.

cannot pass through. Such water as does seep into the suit through the ankles and wrists becomes quickly warmed by the body which adds to the insulating effect. The material usually comes in three thicknesses – 4 mm, 5 mm and 6 mm – and in all cases needs some form of reinforcing. The thinnest variety is not strong enough for caving and rips easily, being more suitable for aquatic sports, rather than the hard life in a cave. Suits made from unlined material require the body to be covered with French chalk or talc to help get them on and off. The 6 mm suit tends to be stiffer but it is the most rugged and has a longer life when reinforced with a nylon lining which reduces the risk of tearing. Another decision to make is whether to choose a mesh or smooth finish – it makes no difference to the price in most cases. Mesh resists creasing and is more snag-resistant as well. A double-lined suit has nylon fabric on both sides and is even more snag-resistant and, as there is a colour range for the double-lined, these will give extra appeal. But they are all quite expensive items of equipment and the cost can be minimised by do-it-yourself make-up kits which require scissors, glue – and patience. To complete the ensemble, neoprene bootees or socks, and hoods are also available. For caving purposes, wet suits also need reinforcing at the knees and elbows where they get the greatest wear and tear. If you go the whole hog and get the lot – jacket, trousers, socks and hood, you can expect to pay around £60 at the time of writing.

Finally, the well-dressed caver needs something on his feet. Woollen knee-length socks are good for warmth and so are the neoprene socks I have mentioned. As to the basic footwear, I have seen people caving in plimsolls, track shoes and riding boots – all quite unsuitable. Caving boots probably have to withstand the hardest treatment ever given to footwear involving long periods of immersion, battering against rock, grinding in sand and mud and often ill-treatment when being dried off. Ordinary fell boots would not last the strain for long but here again, the purpose-built boot is now on the market. Phil Brown of Caving Supplies at Buxton has designed one which comes as near to the ideal as one is likely to get – the Enduro caving boot with double-screwed Commando soles (the best all-round sole) and using non-rotting polyester stitching and laces. A steel toe-cap is an asset, since it is the part of the boot which suffers most in crawls, rubbing against rocks on vertical ladder pitches or jamming in crevices. In addition, the steel toe-cap protects the toes when loose boulders drop on the feet. The National Coal Board miner's boot is also well up to caving standards. My friends at Whernside Manor cave centre have themselves made an excellent contribution to caving footwear with their Whernside 'Welly' and their caver's boot, the product of much research by the warden 'Ben' Lyon. The 'Welly' is a sturdy Wellington boot but with the Vibram or Commando sole and reinforced toe caps. The caver's boot is likewise made of strong rubber with a similar sole to the 'Welly'. Some

Special suits are also available, such as PVC on nylon used successfully on several expeditions, the Spock suit supposedly based on the one-piece tunic of the long-eared crew member of the star ship *Enterprise* in the Startrek TV series, and the Ghar Parau waterproof boiler suit designed for the expedition to the cave of that name in the Zagros Mountains of Iranian Kurdistan. The Ghar Parau suits, now commercially available, are made from synthetic material with inside pockets, elasticated wrists and ankles and a long zip, instead of buttons protected by a Velcro material overlap. Perhaps the greatest contribution to comfort and survival in recent years is the wet suit. This is made from foam rubber sheeting known technically as expanded neoprene and is designed to keep the wearer warm whether in or out of water. The insulation quality arises from the millions of tiny sealed bubbles which do not absorb moisture like a sponge and water people object to rubber because of sweating feet but this is the exception rather than the rule in caving experience. My own personal foot problem is that I have a big one and a little one and, despite many years of trying, I have been unable to find a caver the other way round from myself so that I could arrange a swap or two one-legged cavers of appropriate sizes who might buy a pair and want to throw the other one away! It is ten to one I would get someone the wrong way round. I once advertised in *The Times* for someone who might be my opposite with a big left and a little right – but I got only one reply – from a woman. Even my friends in Stockport Odd Feet Association have been unable to solve this problem for me. However, I digress. Anyway, avoid boots with clip-over hooks for lacing as the hooks catch on the wires of metal ladders and they are often all too easily bent in the threshing about that is sometimes necessary to make progress. Boots with D-rings for laces are not very satisfactory either and the old eye-hole type is undoubtedly the best. Nylon or polyester laces are best for tying – leather becomes brittle and snaps.

What I call optional extras are gloves. Industrial gloves are of use in protecting the hands when hauling loads or lowering equipment, or in preventing cuts and abrasions when using wire ladders. There are also special belay gloves designed to give a positive grip under wet or dry conditions and which provide protection against friction burns when abseiling.

Additional articles of personal equipment have increased in the past few years. At one time a waistband with a karabiner or the *baudrier* chest harness were considered to be quite adequate, and still are, for the less exacting trips. There are many specialised manufactured versions of these on the market designed to give greater comfort and safety. My friends at Troll Products of Uppermill, Oldham, who have been beavering away using their own climbing and caving experience to produce a wide variety of excellent gear, have their own versions of waist and chest fastenings adapted with caving in mind. The Whillans sit-harness, first evolved for climbing, is now widely in use underground, minus various bits and pieces which are extraneous to caving requirements. They also produce a chest and sit-harness designed by Caving Supplies of Buxton for Single Rope Techniques. Less compli-

cated, and adequate for most trips, is their caver's belt which has a non-slip buckle system, the fastening instructions of which must be closely followed if it is to work successfully. A recent development of leg loops converts this into a sit-harness with the advantage that it can be removed in tight crawls. These belts, incidentally, are made from polyester for use only with acid batteries, and nylon for use only with alkali batteries. At the same time, it is also worth bearing in mind that polyester stretches less under load than nylon and is not as suitable as nylon for absorbing a high energy shock load of a leader falling, although this is probably less likely to happen in caving than climbing situations. But polyester has the advantage that its strength loss when wet is minimal as against up to 20 per cent in nylon. There are, of course, various other types of waist and chest harnesses – Petzl, Mole, Rocksport, etc.

I will refer to the various gadgets for ascending and descending in chapter 5 but personal equipment includes the karabiner or snaplink as a means of attachment. There is a wide variety, all of high breaking load, whether of steel or alloy. There are many famous and reputable makes in this field which have been recently joined by a new generation of Maillon rapide links. The screwgate types are the most secure as the locking screw prevents any accidental opening. Fortunately, there are few, if any ex-War Department surplus karabiners around now. These were notoriously unsafe and have been known to fail with loads as low as 300 lb (136 kg).

Other items of personal equipment should include a whistle with which to give signals. Various small tools are also useful – pliers, screwdriver, tin opener; and so is a small personal first aid outfit catering for cuts, burns, headaches and the like. But no alcohol. The amount of everything to be carried is determined by the type of trip and the estimate of how long it will take. Some of the equipment may be carried conveniently on the person and there are several types of gear carrying bags available for caving.

These items, then, are what one needs personally to assemble. The other equipment I shall describe will be in its context of special use or what should be provided by a group or club.

23 Old-style caver heavily burdened with hemp rope ladder and safety line.

4
HORIZONTAL TECHNIQUES

It may well be that the theme of this book is that of survival, of safe caving and taking care. It is regrettable, but true, that caving gets a bad image when rescues are necessary; the good which accrues from the pastime is rarely mentioned in the press and elsewhere. Caving is, admittedly, dangerous, but the dangers can be reduced by training, the use of the correct equipment and the application of commonsense. In fact, it might be useful to recall the poignant sentences at the end of Edward Whymper's description of that first ascent of the Matterhorn which turned from triumph to tragedy and embittered the remaining years of his life. 'Climb if you will, but remember that courage and strength are naught without prudence, and that a momentary negligence may destroy the happiness of a lifetime. Do nothing in haste; look well to each step; and from the beginning think what may be the end.' Substitute 'cave' for 'climb' and that advice is as sound today as it was nearly a hundred years ago.

The art of caving is the art of taking care and the ability to move safely in an environment alien to Man in the realms of unending darkness. The blackness is absolute. Even on the darkest nights above ground there is usually some light about from stars or reflected glows of street lighting. I often encourage novices on first descents to turn out their lights just to appreciate what true darkness is really like. It can be a frightening experience. It is in this environment that the caver must have many skills in order to explore and survive. The novice must master the tools of his trade and their application: how to tie the right knots, how to fasten belays and safety lines, how to fix pegs and bolts, how to fix ladders and ropes for Single Rope Techniques and use the various gadgets associated with them.

A caver needs many of the skills of a rock climber, especially in bridging and chimneying, plus the ability to crawl and wriggle through tight places. A caver should also be able to swim. I know many who cannot and think swimming is unnecessary but water is met with so often underground in streams, lakes, pools and sudden floods that only familiarity with swimming will remove that element of panic which develops in people unused to water.

The best way to learn all the correct techniques of caving is to join a reputable club or, better still, to take one of the special training courses available at outdoor centres or the Whernside Cave and Fell Centre at Sedbergh in Cumbria. The centre at Whernside Manor was originally run by the Scout Association and faced a crisis in 1976 when the Association was unable to meet the annual running costs. A great deal of effort went into the fight for the continuance of the centre and it is now under the aegis of the Yorkshire Dales National Park. As Britain's only full-time caving centre it has a justifiably high reputation throughout the world of caving and offers tuition in all branches of speleology under acknowledged experts.

Most of the larger and more efficient caving clubs have graduate training courses to educate budding cavers to the right standards of proficiency. All of them stress the essential teamwork involved, since caving involves working with others and sharing responsibility for each other's welfare and safety. It should never be attempted alone or without the proper equipment. But as in mountaineering, there is a growing cult of the solo effort which may achieve the ultimate in personal satisfaction. There are some super-cavers well able to undertake single-handed missions, fully aware of the risks and the narrow margin of survival. My only thoughts about it are that it could encourage emulation by the less competent and several loners have either lost their lives or had to be rescued under ignominious circumstances – so the advice of all instructors to never cave alone still stands.

There is a vast amount of literature aimed at the novice and, for many years, there have been handy guide books available for all the caving regions of Britain. The guides, alas, rarely keep pace with the latest explorations, but they do give a broad – although not always accurate – description. New discoveries, changes in access permission or structural alterations in certain passages for various reasons, are circulated throughout club literature or the excellent magazines of the caving world, *Descent,* and the journal of the BCRA, *Caves and Caving*. As in climbing, there is a gradation system which follows pretty well the old climbing nomenclature (caving does not seem to require the higher subtleties of grading used nowadays by European and American climbers).

In the guides, caves and potholes are classified as Easy,

A caver must be prepared to encounter water on his underground sojourn. Stop Pot boulder choke, Easegill Caves, Yorkshire. *John Forder*

Moderate, Difficult, Very Difficult, Severe and Super Severe, an arbitrary arrangement indeed, but it works fairly well. There has also been an attempt to introduce a simplified numerical system using Roman numerals I to V to indicate Moderate, Difficult, Very Difficult, Severe and Super Severe, with a plus or minus as a harder or easier version of the main grade. It is usual for a beginner to be taken through the grades on an ascending scale of difficulty. Unfortunately, in recent years controversy has raged throughout organised caving in Britain as to whether these guide books should become generally available. The fear has been expressed that they may encourage the inexperienced to make their own forays and lead to vandalism (alas, the underworld is just as prone to stupid, wanton acts of

damage) and perhaps create further problems of access by alienating farmers and other landowners whose goodwill is essential to the continuance of the sport. Another fear is that caves of special archaeological interest might be visited by growing hordes and so put them at risk. This is a matter for the caving world but, on balance, I feel that the guides are of value to genuine cavers if used in the right way.

Most novice cavers get a preliminary idea of what to expect by visiting show caves to see the environment under ideal and comfortable conditions. It is also best for beginners to start in a fairly easy cave system with no water hazards, severe drops, loose boulders or doubtful roofs. As a start, nothing more should be attempted than a straight forward walk to gain fam-

25 (left) **Walking in a semi-crouched position at Wilf Taylor's Passage, Lancaster Hole, Yorkshire.** *John Forder*

26 (above) **A tight crawl in Ogof Hesb Alyn, north Wales.** *Sheena Stoddard*

iliarity with some of the obstacles and the general scenery of the underworld. Attention should be paid to the floor and the roof. Loose rocks, unsuspected holes and pools need to be watched for and a careful watch must be kept at head level to avoid unnecessary bumps and bangs to the head and also to miss the various pendant formations which may be damaged by a careless blow.

It takes time for the human eye to accommodate itself to the change from natural daylight to the darkness of a cave and the more limited illumination from one's headlamp. Just inside the zone of darkness, it is a useful tip to close one's eyes for a couple of minutes, standing perfectly still.

Once used to the general cave scenery based on a short ramble underground, the other techniques follow naturally. Some cave passages are lofty and ordinary walking is easy but inevitably various other forms of progress are called for, such as bending, crawling and horizontal wriggling. Walking in a crouched position tends to direct the head downwards and it is useful to try and get a frequent look at the roof of the way ahead for likely obstacles in the way of formations, hanging rocks or dips in the strata. Walking in this semi-crouching position can be tiring and some of the strain can be taken by putting one's hands on the knees or thighs.

Some passageways are known as 'monkey walks' because of the shambling motion of the arm with the weight distributed between the hands and legs. Inevitably, as the roof gets lower, crawling must be resorted to and many cavers find this a painful experience, especially in passages known as knee wreckers. Kneeling on sand or mud is not too bad but there are often long stretches of broken, stony floor with unpleasant protrusions which can hurt that most painful part of the human anatomy, the knee. If it is known that there is to be some lengthy crawling, it is as well to get used to wearing miners' knee pads to protect the joint. Some cavers wear them all the time as they give protection against bumps and bangs in other situations as well and are a useful reinforcement of a vulnerable area of wet suits. Again, when crawling, a quick glance at the way ahead should help one select the best route and spot formations which should be avoided.

Inevitably, even this method ceases to be of use as rock ceiling, walls and floor get closer together to form a narrow tube known as a 'squeeze'. These come in many varieties – rising and falling or twisting in various directions. This is caving at its most claustrophobic – except for water passages and diving. It often takes a long time for a beginner to become confident enough to tackle this sort of problem and frequent practice in fairly easy squeezes is advisable. In theory, where one can pass an arm and one's head along the passageway, the remainder of the body should get through but it should also be borne in mind that it has to come back as well. The one arm extended ahead is useful to pull on an available projection which is in front and also reduces the shoulder width. It is in these

27 (above) The author in a tight, wet 'squeeze' passage.

28 (right) Emerging from a small vertical 'squeeze'. Top series, Ogof Ffynnon Ddu, south Wales. *Sheena Stoddard*

situations that the caver may regret his extra large breakfast or the beer he has had the night before.

At no time try and hurry in a passage like this. Part of the problem is psychological. It takes a real effort of will to force oneself through such a tight situation, aware of the awful confinement of the enclosing rocks. Propulsion may come from the toes or with some kind of a 'shimmy-shake' or serpentine writhing. But if you look like getting stuck, don't go any further as going backwards is often harder than going forwards. It is

here that the thin, wiry caver comes into his own and his more portly brethren sigh – and retreat. The really last-ditch method is to strip off all one's clothing and proceed by what Norbert Casteret called 'reptation' – moving like a snake with a kind of skin action. I've never heard of it being done in a British cave and the potential damage to parts of one's anatomy other than the knee is sufficient to deter most from these extreme measures.

I once had a strange experience in a longish tube in which three of us lay in line astern. Somewhat exhausted and pausing for breath I heard a distinct rhythmic sound rather like that of a water ram – but we were miles from water. Suddenly, I realised that the sound was the heavy beating of our own hearts and that the tube was acting as a kind of giant stethoscope. I drew the attention of this phenomena to my colleagues and a faint voice came up the passage from behind me – 'Proves we're bloody well still alive, doesn't it?' I started to laugh, then realised that even that action had an adverse jamming effect and quickly desisted. When jammed, an inexperienced caver tends to panic and struggles violently, with disastrous results. It is also known that under stress, the body has a certain amount of peripheral expansion, a slight swelling, which can aggravate the problem.

People can become psychologically stuck. If they have little experience they quite fatalistically accept that they are wedged for ever and lose the will to do anything about it. This is where the skill of an able team leader is needed to coax the victim out of his or her inertia and to assist in the moves of extrication. In theory, the same body having gone through a certain space should be able to come back again. Exhaling, pulling and pushing (that is if someone is on either side of the squeeze) is usually sufficient to get out of the predicament. This kind of thing can be avoided if the novice is carefully trained in getting through tight places until he is physically and mentally prepared to cope with the problem.

Other problems arise, as of getting gear through these sections and it may be pushed ahead, which is not always advisable in case it falls down a hole in the floor, or it may be dragged on a cord fastened to one's foot. Sometimes it is best for someone to get through and haul the tackle while a second person backs up by pushing. In tight crawls and squeezes the position of one's accumulator or pocket battery and the position of the wiring is also important. Getting the wire snagged is both frustrating and dangerous. This is where the acetyline lamp is an advantage, up to a point, as it has no trailing wires, although it does pose other risks inherent when in use in a confined space.

Water is, inevitably, met with frequently underground as the greatest formative factor in nearly all cave systems. It is both the caver's friend and his potential enemy. Underground, it is met with in the form of waterfalls, rivers, streams and droplets. In many instances, water passages are shallow enough to be traversed by paddling or wading. This seems innocuous enough but the caver should always be wary of unexpectedly deep flooded rifts in the apparently flat bed. Similarly with underground lakes which may seem wadable but give way to great gulfs. Usually, these hazards are known to a well-trained leader and he can prompt the novice as to their existence. In some places, where these rifts are known, such as Ogof Ffynnon Ddu in south Wales, a traverse was created on balancing poles over the deeper rifts. As cavers often have a perverted sense of humour, I was not given this intelligence on my first trip and submerged, acquiring the nickname of the Submarine due to my ability to disappear under water with great rapidity. When I first started caving, the theory was that water would not go through skin, but later there came a procession of various forms of suiting to help cope with water. Inevitably, a lot of it was from the last war, including inflatable rubber suits which gave non-swimmers every confidence. They were fine until they got a puncture, and the ultimate today are the various forms of wet suits (referred to in chapter 3). Swimming in caving equipment is extremely strenuous but it is well worth mastering as an essential part of an all-round technique. Inflatable dinghies are also used in the wider and longer stream and lake passages, especially where they are of great or uncertain depth. The danger to these lies in the many sharp edged sub-aquatic projections which could lead to a disastrous puncture. 'Boating' in Yugoslavia did not have this hazard, I found. At the time, as inflatable dinghies were luxuries which my Slovenian caving friends there could not afford, they devised a craft slightly larger than an orange box and covered it with plastic. Like the coracle, it took some mastering.

Wherever water is met, it should be treated with respect. In all water passages, always keep an eye on the water level and be prepared to retreat at the first signs of a significant rise unless you are in a cave where there are emergency provisions and facilities for a bivouac, or a safe, alternative high-level route. It is incredible the speed with which water can rise after a sudden storm or a flash flood in the hills. I have been in situations where a fairly easy journey down a stream passage has turned into an immense struggle to survive battling against a rising torrent. I once took a series of photographs (someone else lost my negatives) of a flood in Derbyshire which completely filled a valley within an hour, totally drowning the entrance to a cave where, hopefully, we had a dig and which we vacated hurriedly. It was such a flood which was responsible for the worst disaster in British caving when six cavers, all experienced from the Leeds University Union Speleological Society, died. The force of the water disintegrated their equipment and, when the bodies were eventually found, they were utterly compressed in narrow parts of the system. Once the waters started rising from the Mossdale Beck, they were doomed. Controversy over the incident raged for some time afterwards; Mossdale always had a reputation for swift flooding. The incident tragically underlined the need for cavers to study weather reports and weather conditions over a period before a descent. In some areas, flooding has been accelerated by new drainage on the surface which has speeded the run-off water underground.

Cave diving will be dealt with in chapter 7 as it requires specialist techniques and equipment. But travelling horizontally often brings the caver into areas where a certain amount of ducking or free-diving is necessary to continue. Broadly speaking, a duck is where the rock does not quite reach the water, or, if it does, it is only for a short distance. In passing a duck, the breath need only be held for a few seconds. It needs nerve and training for this total immersion even for only a short time. It is done only when the distance through is well known. Sometimes conditions for a duck have to be created by bailing into dams which have to be specially built.

In such cases, it is necessary to leave someone on the entry side to re-bail as the inevitable seepage refills the air space created. A true sump has the water up to the roof and may stretch for a few feet or may be a completely flooded system extending possibly for miles. Some sumps are short enough to allow a free-dive but there is controversy as to the extent a caver should undertake this. A guide line or wire is certainly necessary but it cuts the margin of survival to an absolute minimum. It does not need much imagination to realise what would happen if a free-diver was only slightly delayed in his passage to new air – a snag on the rock, any misjudgment of distance or even an under-realisation of one's own lung capacity and it is almost certain death. It is one thing to swim 20 yards (18 metres) or more under water in a well-lit and heated public swimming bath and yet another in the dark confines of a cave passage. Argument will always rage in caving and climbing circles as to what is a justifiable risk in the interests of exploration or advancement. One never knows how much risk is involved when a person attempts the feats of a superman.

Apart from the straightforward risk of drowning, free-diving enhances another danger, that of carbon dioxide. It is known that in some caves, fortunately in very rare instances, there are places off the main air flow, or those which are cut off from ventilation by water, where bad air – a build up of CO_2 – occurs. A free-diver is in severe trouble if, on reaching the limits of his lung power, he surfaces in a passage or airbell of stagnant air and takes a deep inhalation. The carbon dioxide may be above the safe upper tolerance limit of 5000 parts per million and this can cause rapid deterioration – physical weakness and giddiness with coma ensuing in high concentrations. This is thought to have been the main factor in the deaths of three members of Newcastle University Caving Club in May 1976 in a party of six attempting the extremely severe transit from Langstroth Pot in Upper Wharfe-

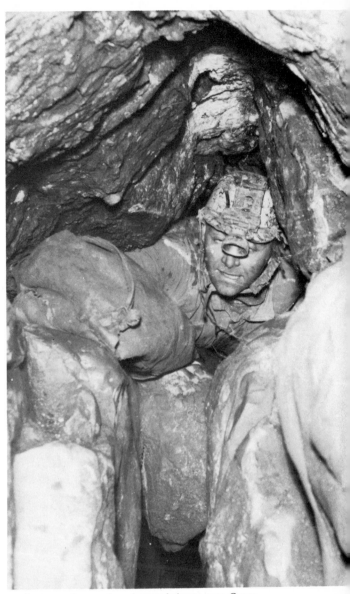

29 Just enough room for a human being to pass. Caver Bernard Chandler struggling through with his tackle bag, south Wales.

dale to Langstroth Cave. To do this the sumps on the way to the cave entrance had to be free-dived and the theory was advanced that the tragic three emerged into an airbell which had a high concentration of carbon dioxide. There they probably either passed out, were so disorientated or weakened that they succumbed to drowning.

Sumps should never be dived alone – i.e. by one member of a party who may have broken away from the others. The most experienced person should go through first, checking guide lines etc., and another experienced person should stay behind so that there is

capable help on each side of the sump. It goes without saying that at least one person in the party should have some knowledge of artificial respiration.

Bad air in caves is still a subject for more scientific data and it is hard to detect just by smell alone. The more usual signs of its presence can be indicated by its effect on a naked flame such as a candle, match or carbide light. If the slightest suspicion of its presence is felt, then departure from the location into the main air flow should be done as soon as possible before discomfort becomes a real problem. And it is a situation most likely to be met with in horizontal passages, especially old mines, rather than in vertical shafts.

30 (left) Spout Hall, Easegill Caves in Yorkshire. *John Forder*

31 (above) A low crawl in Arctic Norway. Note the water line when the cave is flooded.

VERTICAL TECHNIQUES

I have already mentioned that there has been a revolution in the caving world following the evolvement of new techniques and purpose-made equipment – a far cry from the days of ASP (All Spare Parts) caving. The biggest single development has been the growth of SRT – Single Rope Techniques with just one rope being used for descent *and ascent*. This has meant the evolution of a whole breed of new ropes – ordinary climbing ropes will not do because of their stretchability – and also a significant change in caving philosophy. The older generation of cavers who were brought up on the tradition of the ladder – rope or wire – and the belayed lifeline safeguarding the person on the ladder, looked askance at what was an insidious intrusion from the United States but which was later to take the caving scene in Britain by storm.

There was nothing entirely new about using just one rope – many shafts of moderate depth were climbed on a knotted rope which was fine if one's grip did not give out. As with so many aspects of caving and its assortment of equipment, the basic idea came from mountaineering. The need to get off the big Alpine climbs quickly due to bad weather or other factors led to the abseil or rappel in which the friction of the rope crossed over the body was the means of controlling the speed of descent. With the development of the karabiner or metal snap link, the method was improved as this was brought into the frictional scheme of things either from the waist or a simple loop-seat clipped into the crotch. Then followed various forms of descenders – figures-of-eight (two eyelets of metal, not to be confused with the knot) tridents and the like, basically braking systems. Then, climbers forced off a route by weather, shortage of food or equipment etc. became loth to start all over again to reach their ultimate point and thought up the technique of climbing up a rope left in place, to resume where they had left off.

In the early 1930s, the Austrian climber Dr Karl Prusik applied his mind to the problem of retrieving climbers trapped in crevasses and who were unable to climb back due to overhanging and sheer ice. In some cases deaths had occured when the lifeline badly crushed the chest of the victim (in some respects this risk still exists today with some types of harness). Dr Prusik developed the sliding knot on a fixed rope. When freed of weight and tension the knot slides along

the rope but it jams firmly when weight is applied. By using ropes attached to the rescue rope by means of the Prusik knot with looped stirrups for the feet, the ascent was made by alternately standing in one stirrup and sliding the other upwards. The stirrup ropes, threaded through a waist karabiner, helped to keep the body upright. Inevitably cavers, who had always borrowed something from mountaineering, began to see possibilities for such techniques especially in the deeper shafts of the United States and Europe. Britain lagged behind somewhat because our native gulfs have fewer places of such depths where ladders were quite adequate. This knot and its variants is still useful today, so much so that some proponents of SRT insist that novices should be trained in their use right from the start for such occasions as when mechanical ascending equipment fails, gets lost or is otherwise unavailable.

Cavers today face a bewildering variety of gadgets and it would be impossible, within the compass of this book, to refer to them all or substantiate the claims of the many manufacturers and inventors who now dominate the caving scene. The emphasis is on speed and SRT developed primarily in the United States, France and Australia out of the need to hasten the exploration of the big shafts, or pits, as the Americans call them, and thus be able to accomplish more within the short space of time which cavers have available for their sport. Controversy inevitably rages as to whether the end justifies the means or the means will become an end in themselves in Man's attempt to break world records. Already in the Soviet Union there are rock-climbing races! I also know one Derbyshire caver whose passion is no longer for exploration – he prefers to shoot down and up vertical shafts like a yo-yo. Inevitable, I suppose in a world where there is instant acclaim (and not a little money) for the record breaker. Dr Prusik's simple rescue device led, in the mountaineering world, to the acceptance and the creation of gadgets to take climbers back to the points they had left in order to resume the climb. The danger is that it could encourage the less expert to attempt feats beyond his or her ability and strength.

That being said, SRT has come to stay and has a

32 Prusiking the 100 foot (30 metre) pitch in Meregill Hole, Yorkshire. *Sheena Stoddard*

33 (left) Prusik practice in Alum Pot, Yorkshire. *Sheena Stoddard*

34 (above) **Just a few of the gadgets and ropes used nowadays.**

rightful place in caving. It can eliminate the need for large teams and vast amounts of equipment; it enables larger teams to achieve more in their time underground and be of invaluable assistance in cave rescue. Or, in the case of the superbly trained Dave Elliott, who has made important contributions to cave photography and tough techniques, it can lead to solo trips such as his first one-man traverse in two days of the immensely hard Maskhill Mine-Oxlow Cavern-Giant's Hole system in the Peak District. He would be the first to point out that this is a trip which requires the highest competence and fitness even with a team and should only be soloed after considerable thought. The lone caver, like the solo climber, has a motivation which others may not understand but that is not to say that it should not be done. Novices should never enter a cave alone, no matter how apparently easy. Even

those with some degree of competence such as Brian Andrew Kerr, a twenty-year-old Leeds art student, can come unstuck. He went into Goyden Pot in Nidderdale in December 1957 on a solo trip. He had pushed his luck once before in this extremely severe system, which is prone to flooding. This time his luck ran out and he disappeared. Two months later, searchers found mute relics of his trip – one boot, sweaters, rucksack, food tins and a water bottle. He had been careful to put down marker arrows to show him the way back – a journey he was destined never to make.

Most descents require muscle, fitness and nerve. The most congenial way of going down is on a powered winch such as that which has delighted summer visitors to Gaping Gill. The speed of descent often depends on the sense of humour of the winch operator

35 Modern equipment – wire ladders, spreaders and latest rope for SRT.

or whether one lingers on the return in the cooling waters of the Fell Beck. I am glad to say that caving has so far resisted complete mechanisation, since motorised winches are generally too heavy to transport over rough terrain. Winches and their ancillary equipment are prone to break down. I well remember the sadness of Jo Delteil as he told me how his friend Marcel Loubens died in a fall in the Pierre St Martin due to a defect in the parachute harness equipment attaching him to the winch cable. I think I can claim one of the oddest ways of raising people and equipment on the occasion of the expedition to the Spluga della Preta in

Italy. The expedition's hand-operated winch broke down and the huge, heavy Italian wire and wood ladder had become a tangled mass. So a line was tied to my old Ford Capri which I had managed to park close to the entrance of the abyss and, by dint of rough driving, people were towed to the surface.

I will now deal with the traditional means of descent which are recommended for novices coming into a caving environment for the first time. The descent is done on electron ladders made of wire with lightweight metal staves. These have completely replaced

36 The old winch and cradle means of descending Gaping Gill. *News Chronicle, Manchester*

inch spacing obviously means fewer rungs and, with less metal involved, these ladders are accordingly cheaper. Whichever is chosen, it is wisest to standardise on one or the other – either 10 or 12 inch spacing. It is a bit disconcerting to link ladders with differing spaces between the rungs – the 2 inch (5 cm) difference can affect climbing rhythm which is important on long pitches. There are, of course, other ladder lengths, the Continental ones usually coming in $5\frac{1}{2}$ metres and 10 metres. The manufacturers of these ladders have reached high standards but individuals or clubs may make their own in lengths, rung diameters and spacing suitable to their needs.

A recent study by Brian Paul Hindle of the British Cave Research Association has brought some refreshing thought to consideration of the optimum lengths for caving ladders and ropes. He makes the valid point that in many instances, particularly in the Pennines, quite large amounts of waste ladder and rope, superfluous to requirements, are carried. There is a case for a combination of ladder lengths which would more adequately meet the needs of any exploration. Apart from familiarisation with ladders, it is also important to make regular inspections of them, cleaning off all mud and grit. Corrosion is a possibility and must be guarded against. A broken rung or a snapping wire means disaster unless there is a lifeline in use. Today the tendency is to omit certain safety factors – I've been guilty of it myself – on what appear to be superficially easy pitches, but such short cuts can also mean shortened lives.

The correct rigging of a ladder is the first stage in its use, involving carefully uncoiling it and attaching it to the belay point firmly before lowering it over the edge. There have been cases of someone letting go of the top end before it has been fixed. If it is the only ladder in the party, it can be the end of the trip in some instances. A party leader must ensure that the ladder is affixed securely, usually with a tape sling clipped to a spreader which ensures that the top of the ladder maintains its standard width. Belaying may be over a knob of rock, formation (to be avoided wherever possible), expansion bolts, short lengths of crowbar driven into the rock, beams (if unrotted) or, as I have used successfully, a short length of railway line wedged firmly over the top of a shaft. Some caves and potholes have permanently fixed belay points and even fixed ladders but these should never be used without close inspection and testing. It is no use blaming other people's inadequacies if things go wrong and it is better to affix one's own security system. Joining other lengths of wire ladder is quite simple with the aid of metal C rings of appropriate strength.

It takes experience to get the feel of a correctly rigged ladder. Every effort should be made to get the twists out of a ladder as it is suspended down a shaft because a twist, if it is tight against the rock wall, can be difficult to negotiate. It does not matter quite as much if the

the wood and rope variety, being easier to rig and carry. I think ladders will remain in basic use for a long time yet, no matter what other methods are exploited. They are probably best for the shorter pitches in any event, and their use, together with a lifeline, should be part of the basic training of novice cavers. Familiarisation should first take place above ground in the techniques of applying belays, fixing ladders and joining ladders together. Ladder lengths vary and, despite metrication, at the time of writing the standard length is usually 25 feet ($7\frac{1}{2}$ metres) with either 10 or 12 inch (25 or 30 cm) spacing between the rungs. The 12

37 Heavy-duty hand winch in use on the Spluga della Preta, Italy.

ladder hangs freely in an open situation. Holding the ladder out at arm's length and shaking it often suffices to get the twists out. With a novice party, an experienced caver should be first down and there should be an experienced person at the top as well. The first man down (or woman – there is a growing number of fine women cavers around today) should unwind any twists or get the ladder free if it has snagged on anything or bunched up on a ledge. Lifelining should be done from a separate belay point. Again, the attachment depends on the terrain, the anchorage can either be natural or artificial but if it has been fixed there for some time, it needs checking or ignoring in case of doubt. The lifeliner may be attached to this belay by slings of tape of suitable strength or the inactive part of the lifeline, the process being completed with a screwgate karabiner which ensures no accidental opening of the gate.

In the mountaineering world there are many systems for holding a falling leader – they proliferate as in caving – some useable only with certain types of rope. But for basic ladder work the simple tie-on with a karabiner is adequate when attached to the person on

the ladder either by a nylon waist sling or a sit-harness (of which more anon). The simplest tie-on knot for this purpose, and still extremely effective in caving, is the good old bowline remembered by many by the mnemonic of the rabbit popping out of its hole, going round the tree and popping back down the hole again. This describes somewhat colourfully putting a loop on the rope, taking the end through it and round the standing rope, threading it back through the hole and then tightening. Its tightness may be easily adjusted and it may be made even more secure with an overhand knot. Another useful and easy knot is the figure-of-eight for attachment to the belay. The figure-of-eight knot looks exactly as its name implies and is one of the oldest and most versatile knots in existence, useful both for anchoring and joining two ropes together. For the latter purpose, it is stronger and better than the sometimes recommended fisherman's knot which is simply two overhand knots on the separate ropes pulled together in opposition. Another popular, but more complicated knot, was evolved by a member of my own climbing club, Ken Tarbuck, for securing a stance. Its main advantage is that it grips the rope in such a way that it acts as a shock absorber and reduces the sudden jerk which may cause breakage. It is a knot which requires the greatest care in tying and must be correctly finished with a figure-of-eight knot to stop the free end running through.

Quite clearly, the lifeliner must not be pulled from his position and the stance taken must not be casual. Sometimes, on a short pitch, it may be adequate for the lifeliner to jam into position or brace his feet against an opposing wall or boulder, but I still feel it is safest to be tied, so that a sudden fall cannot bring disaster. The stance should be so that the rope passes round the body with one hand controlling the uncoiling rope and the other directing it down the shaft. Preferably one hip should be braced forward and the lifeline passed above the anchor ropes with one complete turn around the controlling forearm (from inside to outside – never under any circumstances on the directing arm). The controlling forearm is braced against the thigh and the braking is done with that hand and arm. Rotating the wrist on the controlling forearm and the pressure of the hand are part of the braking system and further energy and shock is absorbed in the body, again reducing the sudden jerk. This rope work with the appropriate knots should be taught and practised to perfection before a novice goes underground.

Moreover, before a novice makes a descent, he should be taught the correct whistle and rope signals which act as a guide to the lifeliner when he may not be able to hear shouted instructions. One blast or one pull on the rope means: Stop paying out the rope. Two blasts or two tugs on the rope means: Take in the rope. Three blasts or three pulls means: Continue to pay out the rope. One long blast or a long, continuous pull means: An emergency, hold tight. A sensitive lifeliner can often feel whether the person on the ladder is in trouble. Care should be taken not to accumulate slack so that if the person on the ladder falls, it comes with a jerk on the rope and then on the lifeliner. A lifeliner can often gauge the rhythm of a descent or a climb and pay out rope or take it in accordingly.

For the actual descent on the ladder, two methods are used. On rope ladders with wooden staves, the simple way is to climb on it with both feet from the front, pushing them on to the rungs from the front and gripping the rope sides of the ladder from behind with the hands crossed over each other. This helps to keep the body upright. The main thing is to keep as upright as possible, otherwise the tendency is for the feet to push the ladder away, the strain (which is considerable) comes on one's hands and forearms, quickly causing tiredness, and a large area of the body leans backwards over the gulf on which gravity can take its toll.

On the electron ladder the best technique is to 'make love' to it. That is, to cross the hands behind and grip the rungs, one hand over the other, and to have one foot on the front of the ladder seeking purchase from the front and the other round the back of the ladder with the heel slotting on to the rung from behind. This applies of course where the ladder is hanging freely in space down a shaft. When it is close against a rock wall, both toes must enter the rung from the front and a kicking movement of the foot backs the ladder away from the wall. If the foot is pushed right up to the instep, this holds the next rung away from the rock so that the other foot can be inserted in it. Try always to get the foot in as far as the instep in such a position that it reduces the risk of cramp in the calf and slipping if only nebulous toe-holds are used.

Going over the edge where the ladder is tight against the rock is another problem, and it is as well to have some of the strain taken on a tight rope from the lifeliner while you pull the ladder away in order to get a purchase. At this stage, the rungs can be held from the front until there is sufficient free space to adopt the behind-hand-and-foot technique.

Frequent practice either from a beam in a gymnasium, the branch of a tree, against the side wall of some building or outside rock face helps to give the confidence so necessary for ladder work. Remember always to try and keep the body as vertical as possible. Many novice cavers, like novice climbers, try to climb entirely with their hands and arms, which is exceedingly tiring and generally useless. Keeping the body upright spreads the load through the great lifting muscles of the thighs and small of the back. By distributing the weight and lifting or descending load in this fashion, more muscle groups are brought into play and fatigue is greatly diminished.

Seek an even rhythm of movement and try not to move in a series of tense jerks. The perfect caver seems to flow up and down a ladder but it takes practice to pass from the first gentle struggle on a 20 foot (6 metre) pitch to the 300 foot (91 metre) main shaft of Gaping Gill.

Do not hesitate to rest if you tire. Sometimes it is possible to step off the ladder on to a convenient ledge where you can get a second wind and build up steam for another section of the climb. If there is no ledge, clip on to the ladder with the karabiner and this is where the chest harness or rope baudrier is a boon as this keeps the centre of gravity higher and causes less strain if you have to let go and just dangle. The waist-loop tends to crush up the bottom of the rib cage in such circumstances and also increases the possibility of toppling upside down.

The greatest strain naturally comes when ascending the ladder, and the lifeliner must sense when a good strong pull is necessary. Care must be taken not to tug too hard as this can upset the rhythm of a climber or pull him off altogether. If a man is too exhausted to climb, a separate rope may be used – if he is not too far gone to assist his upward journey with, if possible, a hauling party separate from the lifeliner who must continue his function.

Incidentals to ladder work include the careful working-out of a programme. Sometimes, a man may

be left in a 'sentry-box' or some other convenient belay point to await the return of the others in the party and assist and protect their ascent. This is a long, boring job for somebody and it is often preferable for all the party to go down. To do this safely, the lifeline is threaded through a pulley, preferably from the ladder anchor point. The lifeline passes through the pulley block and the lifeliner can tie on and be lifelined from the bottom of the pitch or pothole by a second man who must also be secured by the basic anchor technique. Every care must be taken that when the last man down reaches bottom, the two ends of the lifeline be joined together so as to form a continuous loop. Losing the end which may whip up through the pulley could mean that someone would have to climb the ladder unprotected to re-establish the belay. Some have done this but it is bad practice. The rope through the pulley block must be fixed at the bottom of the pitch so that it may be used for lifelining the first man back up. If the expedition is big enough it is best to let two or three of the more experienced go up first with an experienced person left to the last. In this way, the less expert going up in between can be given every assistance as a man below the ladder can see many of the snags which a man on the ladder may be running into.

Apart from getting cavers up and down shafts, ladders may be used in various ways, such as making an aerial tightrope above an awkward waterfall. This can be done by suspending a section of ladder between one fixed point and another horizontally and balancing along it using another rope as a hand rail and a lifeline for any emergency. But inevitably, the laddering of a waterfall cannot be avoided. This requires no difference in technique, only greater care, because the water pressure can sweep a climber off a ladder and the unending drumming sound can have a bemusing effect.

Concluding the subject of ladders, the final problem of all is getting them back out of a shaft. This can be done in a number of ways. The last man up the shaft can tie a spare line to the end of the ladder and it can be brought up while he is climbing on a higher section of it so that he is on hand to guide it around any snags which may occur. Or he can fasten it to his own waistband or a short length of line, trailing it behind him as he ascends.

Modern caving throughout the world is now heavily geared to speed of descending and ascending. This brings me to Single Rope Techniques. SRT meant a complete re-evaluation of ropes and equipment. Man-made fibre ropes had already begun to replace the traditional manilla, hemp and sisal ropes which had served so well in the past. These had the disadvantages of bulk and weight which increased immensely when wet and muddy. They also deteriorated rapidly in caving situations and they faded from the scene along with the traditional rope and wooden ladders. Nylon first arrived in the climbing world and quickly followed into caving. Then other thermoplastics were developed with varying degrees of load absorption, frictional melting points, stretchability, anti-spin factors, abrasion resistance and varying standards of deterioration. The question of which rope has always been a controversial aspect of caving and still is. Vying for consideration as the definitive ropes are the two synthetic fibres of nylon, the long-chain polyamide and the straight-chain polyester better known under its trade name of Terylene. Nylon has been rejected by some cavers who contend that it is too elastic and is prone to some degree of weakening when wet. But it has been demonstrated that its strength-loss when wet still leaves it stronger than other man-made fibres even when they are dry. In a long letter to me, Dick Newell, president of Blue Water, the American rope manufacturers (admittedly with a vested interest) contends that nylon in its latest form is still the best material for caving ropes because of its load-shock absorbing qualities. Polyester or Terylene does not lose strength when wet which, for some cavers, tips the balance in its favour.

The other man-made fibre which appeared on the caving scene was the thermoplastic polypropylene which, at one stage looked like taking over in its various configurations known as staple spun, multifilament or fibre film – the different ways of producing the rope. But doubts about this type of rope arose after Britain's first SRT fatality in Gaping Gill in December 1974. David Huxtable of University College, Swansea, was abseiling down the main shaft when he fell to his death nearly 300 feet (91 metres), the rope breaking at a point where it ran over the edge of the rock. Subsequent tests revealed that it was a staple spun hawser polypropylene rope. Two important factors emerged. The rope's low melting point under friction made it vulnerable to weakening and snapping due to abrasion. One test revealed that a rope of this construction used over an edge failed after 35 *seconds* as against the 25 minutes of a nylon rope under comparable conditions of use. The other factor was that in some way Huxtable may have created a small amount of slack or stepped off without slowly tensioning the rope, and the sudden jerk put the critical load on the rope and snapped it. Obviously, then, this type of rope has been condemned as unacceptable in most cave situations where it could come under a shock load.

Ropes generally best for caving should conform to British Standard specifications or, as at the time of writing there is no international caving standard, to those of the Union Internationale des Associations d'Alpinisme. As with mountaineering ropes, caving ropes mainly use the kernmantel system having an inner core within and outer sheath, or braiding. Plain hawser laid ropes which should be at least $\frac{5}{12}$ inch (12 mm) diameter are susceptible to kinking and consequent damage unless regularly untwisted.

38 Using a ladder to enter Manor Farm Swallet, the Mendip Hills. *Sheena Stoddard*

Sheathed ropes tend to reduce spinning and have the strength to withstand continuous strain. It is known, however, that the sheath may shear away from the core with alarming consequences. There is obvious wear and tear from the various devices in use, some more than others. Unless the rope hangs freely over a drop the greatest risk of abrasion arises where the rope, of necessity, must pass over an edge of rock. All ropes should be protected by some form of padding. Water running on to the pitch is also a factor. Manufacturers of ropes for caving purposes are well aware of the dangers and of their responsibilities, and research is still going on to eliminate the risks. Very often, the cost does come into the considerations when purchasing but this is one area where economy can be fatal. It is better to spend a few pounds more on a rope which meets the recognised standards for caving than risk something inferior. There are, of course, ropes not made specially for caving – i.e. marine use which have the useful quality of floatability, but may not always conform to the requirements of caving conditions. Above all, never, ever, buy a second-hand rope as its history of storage, stress in use and general maintenance must always be unknown. There have also been cases where ropes have been stolen and later re-sold, a totally reprehensible and dangerous practice.

As the rope is such a vital part of one's equipment, whether as a personal possession or that of a club, its care is paramount. Only the most responsible and experienced people should become tackle masters because so much depends on them. A new rope should be examined minutely on purchase. Manufacturers do have their own high quality controls – their reputations are at stake as well as your life. Some ropes may have minor bumps in them where the new material is joined in the manufacturing process. I am assured that these make no significant difference to the strength but they may affect the operation of an ascender. A note should be made of the date of purchase and a log kept of its use and the type of equipment used on it. In use, all points of likely abrasion should be padded. Knots should not impair its strength. Equipment should not produce excessive heat due to speed nor should it have rough edges which will cut in. Ropes should be kept clean. Ideally, a rope should be inspected carefully after every trip and this is best done after cleansing. A muddy rope will increase wear on itself as well as equipment. Manufacturers usually give instructions as to cleaning. Some recommend cold water, some lukewarm; never hot. If a mild soap or mild detergent is used, then the rope needs thorough rinsing afterwards. Heat should never be used to dry it, either as hot air, near a fire or stove. There is little harm in a damp rope being hung in well-ventilated conditions but direct, hot sunlight is best avoided. Ropes should be protected from chemical damage – nylon is affected by alkaline, and polyester by acid. Fuel oils of various kinds, paint,

spent carbide and other chemicals have a deteriorative effect.

Examination should be minute for damage of either cuts or thinning of the sheath. The wear on a kern-mantel rope is usually on the sheath, and fuzz which is created by wear may be beneficial in that it tends to form a protective shield for the inner fibres. But, if the slightest doubt is felt, the rope should be pulled out of service and discarded. If so, it would be useful to return it to the manufacturers for their views (something to be learnt from the damage may be useful) or submitted for scrutiny by the National Caving Association equipment committee which does valuable work in this field. To give equal wear over a rope's length, it is also suggested that it should be reversed periodically – hence marking each end with a different colour tag which should also give the length. Some shrinkage in width and length may happen after wetting but this seems not to be significant in its effect on performance. It may even be beneficial when the sheath tightens on the core. Finally, there is no hard and fast rule on how long a rope should be kept. All modern ropes keep well when properly stored and treated benevolently. All depends on the frequency with which a rope is used and the cumulative effect of its active use underground. With ropes climbing towards the £100 per 100 metres mark, the temptation may be to continue using a damaged or worn rope. Don't – funerals are much more expensive.

SRT today involves a great range of gadgets and systems which have varying degrees of safety and performance. Each one has its proponents and opponents and the choice of equipment, in the end, comes down to what suits the individual caver for comfort and facility in use, plus the need for complete protection. Abseiling descents were first made with the rope only long before the various braking devices came into use and it is still possible to do this by one or other of the old classic methods. People who do not want to trust a single rope for hauling themselves out of a shaft are usually quite happy to make an abseil descent and return via the ladder. This hurries things along a bit and the nervous or inexperienced may be protected – indeed, should be protected – with a lifeline as well. In this regard, using ladders and abseil instead of full SRT, self-life-lining came into fashion using a jammer on the safety rope, or a shunt to take the strain and give support in the event of ladder failure. This technique has its merits on short ladder pitches with a limited number in the party where there is no need to leave someone behind for belaying. It is useful for a novice party with an experienced leader. The leader may see the others down the ladder safely and abseil to join the party and self-life-lining on the return to give belay protection for the ladder climbers.

But with full SRT you are completely alone with the rope, your equipment, your muscles and your thoughts. Through the years, the hardware has proliferated greatly with modifications made in the light of

39 Abseiling pitch 3 in Bull Pot, Yorkshire. *John Forder*

experience and the various defects exposed in usage. Descending systems must be effective to control the speed of descent or to stop when necessary. They all involve friction on the rope, all impose wear and tear and all may be affected by dry or wet and muddy conditions. It is rare for any two cavers to agree on anything – the columns of the world's caving journals give ample evidence of this, often in acerbic terms. The best I can do is to describe, in the simplest terms, the equipment available without necessarily plugging the claims of the manufacturers who, in many cases are old caving friends whose hardware is the product of considerable experience.

An early development was the placing of brake bars placed across a karabiner with the rope threaded through and controlled by pressure. This system was cheap but fell into disfavour because of the inherent weakness of karabiners at the gate, the most frequent point of failure. It was also not unknown for even experienced cavers to thread the rope back to front across the bars so that pressure, instead of pulling the brake bar tight on the karabiner, opened the notched slot. The old Alpine trick of using double-crossed karabiners has been used in an emergency but is not a recommended caving technique. A really effective descent control is the figure-of-eight descender (not to be confused with the knot of the same name). Among the most popular in use in this country are made by Clogwyn Climbing Gear, better known as Clog of Deinolen, north Wales. Having spent some time in the factory of Denny Moorhouse I can vouch for the care and workmanship that goes into his products. Figure-of-eights operate with the abseil rope threaded through the larger of two metal eyes, the smaller being attached to the waist karabiner or harness. The running rope is controlled by the hands and, in caving, are generally recommended for descents of up to about 200 feet (61 metres) as they tend to impart a degree of spin, and control is said to diminish on exceedingly long drops. Basic weights are 8 ounces (226 grams), or the lighter alloy with a non-stick coating to reduce wear on wet and dirty ropes, of 4 ounces (113 grams). The Pierre Allain 'trident' and some of the other climbing descending accessories never really caught on, though a variation of the 'trident' has been popular in parts of Australia.

Popular in Europe and with growing devotees in Britain are the bobbin-type descenders devised by that fine French speleologist and pioneer of the scaling-pole, Fernand Petzl, and who now specialises in all types of caving gear, albeit somewhat expensive. With the bobbin descender, in its single or double rope constructions, the rope passes over pulley wheels within an aluminium frame. It may be attached to the caver with just one screw-gate karabiner but greater control and security is given by using two karabiners and a delta maillon rapide for attachment. The rope is safely locked into position. A safety catch prevents accidental opening and a good lock-stop can be made

with the bight, providing it is done correctly. Petzl contends that this method does not impart twist like the figure-of-eight and keeps the rope running straight and bending it gently over the bobbins. Both single and double rope versions have a rapid attachment configuration which enables fixing without touching the karabiner and obviates the risk of dropping the whole thing down the shaft. In any event, it is a wise precaution to secure one's equipment at all times to prevent embarrassing and dangerous separation.

Probably the greatest area of controversy is the use of the rappel or abseil rack as against the whaletail, a disputation which became almost a Northern v. Southern Hemisphere affair. Both were, originally, American contributions to caving, the rack devised by John W. Cole of Huntsville, Alabama, and the whaletail by Gerald A. Wood. The rack came first and its *modus operandi* is an extension of the old brake bar and karabiner rig insofar as it involves a similar principle, except that a greater number of bars are involved

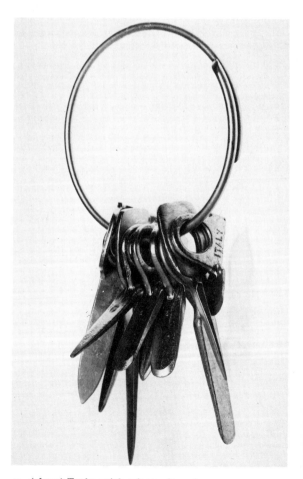

40 (above) Tanky quick-release piton ring.

41 (right) Descending a handline pitch in Lancaster Hole, Yorkshire. *John Forder*

which are placed across a metal frame of elongated U construction with an eye-loop for attachment to the caver's harness. The amount of friction applied depends on the threading of the rope through the bars and this may be varied according to circumstances, such as the caver's weight etc., by reducing or adding to the number of bars or running them in pairs. Through the years various weaknesses, such as bending due to lack of rigidity in the early U frames or the straightening of badly constructed eye-loops, have been overcome particularly with racks like the Curlew with its equilateral U and double-bolted end for greater security. Wear on the bars is inevitable with some alloys subject to grooving due to frictional heat and therefore reduce the contouring of the rope and its braking efficiency. But a big advantage is that rack bars may easily be replaced at no great expense. To meet some of the problems of wear, overheating and the need for various bar adjustments on a long descent, the so-called Super Rack was evolved with thicker 10 inch (25 mm) square bars with a running groove which keeps the rope essentially central. The number of bars on the rack may vary according to the requirements of a given situation taking into account – as with the others – the caver's weight, rope weight and thickness and the length of the descent.

The rival to the rack is the whaletail, much favoured by Australian cavers. It is sturdier in construction, being made from solid aluminium with slots machined into the spine. As with the rack it is possible to change the degree of friction by positioning the rope in a varying permutation of slots. Placing the rope in correctly is an essential part of both systems and it is essential that the whaletail should have a locking safety gate which should keep the rope in at least two slots in the event of it jerking out of the others. It would take a great deal of space to detail the pros and cons of both systems which led to a serious dialogue between Neil Montgomery and John Cole – Neil for the whaletail, John for the rack. I think the conclusion was an honourable draw with Neil's final evaluation that 'both devices are safe and have their advantages, once a caver has become familiar with their proper use.' But if price is a consideration, then the whaletail is certainly more expensive and it is a much more difficult proposition to repair the slots on the whaletail than to replace bars on the rack. Cavers with engineering knowledge and skill in metals can make their own, of course, but few have the high standards required to make this equipment on which so much depends.

Protecting high-speed descents with a safety line is also ruled out for a number of reasons. It would defeat the purpose of SRT in making a swift descent and, because of rope spin, the difficulty of giving signals in rapid transit – even the risk of hanging a caver with a loose coil – lifelining has no place in this form of fast caving. Reliance is inevitably on the control of the descending device but there is some security and increased safety in the use of another Petzl gadget, the shunt, a jammer which may run freely on the rope and lock on or be freed as required in the descent. It is claimed to be suitable for both single and double rope work although there has been some doubt about its efficacy on a single rope due to possible distortion of the cam in the event of a shock load coming suddenly to bear.

Returning up a single rope requires a wide variety of ascending equipment which incorporate locking and freeing attachments to the rope in order to make upwards progress along with footloops or stirrups. Ascenders most generally in use are Jumars developed by Jusy, a Swiss gamewarden, and an engineer called Marti – the first letters of their names being run together; and similar devices made by Clogwyn Climbing Gear and Petzl in France; also ropewalkers of various kinds. Each system gives a variety of means of progress, lifting the body in foot loops using either both legs at once or alternately, or even just one leg at a time. There is at least a score of methods for which cavers may have various degrees of aptitude. All the systems require some form of harness attachment at the waist and chest in which to maintain the body in an appropriate position for climbing, stopping on the rope to undertake various manoeuvres such as passing knots or anchor positions, or just resting. The simplest attachment is the caver's belt which has now virtually superseded rope waist-slings. Leg loops may be attached to make it into a sit-harness. A purpose-designed sit-harness, popular in Britain and elsewhere, is the adaptation of Don Whillans' climbing harness made by Troll of Uppermill, Oldham. As it is made of polyester, it is resistant to acids but is affected by alkilis used in some other batteries. The Whillans harness is extremely effective for prusiking but polyester is obviously not as suitable as nylon for shock loads such as a fall but, generally, the tension of prusiking does not reach this force. Some Continental and American cavers prefer the baudrier or shoulder harness in nylon which eliminates the use of a waist belt and which reduces the risk of abdominal injury in the event of a fall. Chest harnesses, however, do create problems of constriction to the extent of fatal suffocation if the whole body weight is allowed to remain suspended for any length of time and, in this regard the sit-harness is better.

The two main systems in use are rope-walking and sit-stand. Rope-walking is faster and high-speed cavers prefer these methods for that reason. But speed is not always consistent with safety. In the sit-stand system, often called the frog system because of the way one bends the legs and straightens them again to gain height, the body is at rest more often and the system is much easier to use by passing rope joining knots, overhangs and starting and getting off pitches. A variation of the sit-stand method is known as the inchworm in which a foot bar mounted on an ascender is used. Another aid to equilibrium and comfort is the chest-mounted roller box which assists in keeping the body upright and close to the rope, reducing the strains

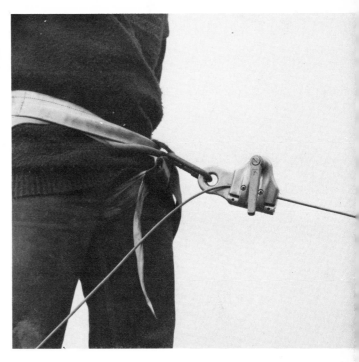

42　Clam Products 'Spider' ascender and descender for use on 5 mm wire rope.

43　Descender on wire.

44　Two ascenders in action with body harness omitted for clarity.

45　Descender in action.

caused by the body being thrust away from the vertical. It is difficult to generalise but the leading authorities recommend rope-walking systems for long, free drops and the sit-stand method on the shorter drops where it may be necessary to cross overhangs or get around knots etc. As Neil Montgomery has pointed out, a compromise choice will need to be made, but he favours the frog system for general cave use.

No summary of the various techniques would be complete without reference to other means of getting up and down apart from single ropes, ladders and winches. It was inevitable that the Americans should turn to some form of mechanised raising and lowering of the body either by a battery-powered operation or some form of petrol engine. The most likely device, invented by Nevin Davis of Pennsylvania and called Motorised Ascending Device, made its appearance in 1969. Not inaptly, it was known as MAD for short and incorporated a one horse power petrol engine with the rope threaded over pulleys. It has been used successfully in deep potholes but seems to have little practical application in this country except for a big open shaft like Gaping Gill. Then, in 1979 Sam Heath, a fine caver and a development engineer who founded Clam Products of Littletown, West Yorkshire, came out with what he claimed to be the world's first independent modular SRT system based on steel wire rope. Called the Spider, it uses 5 mm diameter, 1900 kg, 36 strand non-rotational multi-lay wire. Wire rope of this capacity has many advantages over other rope, especially as it is galvanised to prevent rusting and has none of the inherent weaknesses of rope due to acid and chemical attack. The descent is controlled mechanically and specially hardened gripper cams grasp the rope wire for the ascent. As a practical caver, Sam does not see the Spider as the be all and end all of SRT. As he told me, there may well be applications where the Spider system is unacceptable in a cave and he believes that ladder work and conventional SRT are just as essential caving techniques as any other part of a caver's equipment.

No matter what system is used, all need to overcome the problems of emergencies and the need to switch from abseil to prusik and vice versa. For various reasons a caver may have to reverse direction and this is a major consideration at all times. For this and other reasons, whatever system is used, it must be thoroughly learnt before going underground. The fastening of knots, karabiners, maillon rapides, belts, loops and other attachments should be familiarised before their use in a cave situation. Rope work should be undertaken from some convenient tree or bridge (with permission) so that abseiling, passing knots, intermediate anchors and other obstacles and prusiking, by whatever system, becomes second nature. Rigging pitches is also important and this may be done from convenient rock bollards (formations should be avoided where possible), beams, various metal chocks and bolts with their appropriate hangers. It should be a long time before a beginner is allowed to undertake such rigging anyway, but this aspect of caving is probably the most important of all. A badly fixed bolt, a wrongly placed peg or a sloppily tied knot could mean disaster and no amount of book reading can replace practical application under the guidance of experts.

Fast descending on ropes has problems which tend to be overlooked, such as catching one's clothing in the equipment. Hair in the form of beards and long flowing locks has also been known to get caught, with painful results. Above all, I cannot stress too much that every piece of your equipment should be checked and re-checked before and after use. All mechanical devices are subject to wear, cams become less efficient, some ascenders can fracture when dropped, locking pins may drop out, harnesses and ropes can become weak for many reasons. Minute inspection may make all the difference between a quiet and successful day's caving or a newspaper obituary.

6
OTHER TECHNIQUES

I have covered some of the aspects of getting up and down and traversing across. Other means are also used in conjunction with these, designed to cope with odd and unusual problems which occur underground. Very often, a caving party will come up against a sheer wall rising ahead. Exploration of such a wall may easily lead to a new part of a system, upper passages which may be useful in by-passing flooded sections or providing safety in the event of rising waters. Sometimes it is possible to overcome this obstacle by routine rock-climbing methods, but often the limestone is worn smooth of holds by water. Pegging and the use of etriers is sometimes feasible, which is often well within the skills of well-trained cavers. When this cannot be done, the scaling pole (or maypole) is brought into service.

The reason it is sometimes called a 'maypole' is obvious when the pole is festooned with its rig of ladders and ropes. Like so many other caving innovations it originated in France where Robert de Joly, founder of the Societé Spéléologique de France was probably the first to systematise the various techniques now commonplace today. He was, for instance, the progenitor of the elektron ladder with its light-weight metal rungs and wire sides. He stimulated Pierre Chevalier in the production of the maypole which is made up from light-weight metal sections which join together. The top section usually has a T piece welded on or a special clamp to which may be affixed the ladder and a pulley or runner for lifelining from below, whilst the first ascent is made. The pole should be braced with guy lines and its base wedged with boulders. Further security may be given by a line from the pole to the rock wall attached to a piton or suitable rock bollard to reduce the possibility of the pole being forced away from the rock. Once the first ascent has been made and possibility of further exploration confirmed, the ladder is fixed in the usual way and the pole can be de-sectionalised for further use. It is also now possible to use SRT. Chevalier's earliest explorations using the maypole and ladder technique which he perfected brought success in the famous Trou du Glaz, in the deep limestone of the Dent de Crolles near Grenoble.

It is often necessary underground to make extensive traverses. In some places, this can be done by walking along narrow ledges, hand traversing or penduluming.

46 A Lancashire caver using ordinary rock climbing technique to descend a cave passage in Norway.

A traverse may be made to avoid a stream passage or a lake. Bridging or straddling techniques are also used. Some ledges are satisfyingly large and are no more difficult than walking along a pavement, but some are too narrow and delicate to balance on and it is normal practice to protect these with a rope or wire pegged or bolted into position as a handrail or for clipping on to.

47 (left) Bridging in order to traverse along a meander. Note the plastic water bottle, an important piece of equipment. *Boyd Milligan*

48 (above) Back and knee technique used in climbing a rift or chimney. *Boyd Milligan*

49 Partly natural, partly man-made, a mine passage near Alston, Cumbria. *Peter Jackson*

The insertion of pegs or bolts should never be left to novices. In some caves, these traverse ropes or wire are left *in situ* and cavers are often tempted to use them without thought to testing them. Inspection of these fixed aids is vital before their re-use – bolts and pegs become loose, wires and ropes are subject to wear and tear. It is impossible to check that all the fixtures are safe and, if there is the slightest doubt, it is wisest to make one's own arrangements. In fact fixed aids of all kinds should never be taken on trust and novices should certainly be protected with a lifeline even when making an apparently easy traverse.

Limestone has varying degrees of stability and must always be treated warily because of its nature. Earth movements, erosion, distant explosions from quarrying, even shouting and whistling can bring down a fall of rock. You may dislodge rocks yourself whilst climbing or walking and a warning cry of 'Below' should be given. Rock falls often choke up cave passages with boulders which may lie poised over other boulders or drops. Only one person at a time should

move on a boulder slope. Too many people on a slope may cause an avalanche of rock which, apart from possibly blocking the way, may have disastrous consequences. It was a theory at the time, some twenty years ago, that David Priestman aged eighteen died in the Dowber Gill passage of Dow Cave, because a rock was dislodged as someone traversed above him. It weighed over half a ton and he died instantly when it landed on his head. Other members in the party had also been shouting to each other as they tried to find their way across this tricky route. Some cavers have escaped with nothing worse than a trapped ankle or a jammed knee cap but even these can be serious in a cave.

Loose rocks are also met with in mines. Although man-made, mines can be as complex as caves, a fact which old plans and charts reveal. The great thing is not to use anything left behind in a mine, on trust. Rock walls built up by miners may look solid and safe, but this may not be so. Treat them with care. Nor should you use the old wooden stemples, or iron spikes left behind by miners of old, as it is impossible to tell how safe they are. Some shafts are lined with stones, magnificent examples of the handiwork of these fine old craftsmen, but they are often unreliable for use as hand- and foot-holds and should be treated accordingly. The roofs of these artificially made passages are also suspect and so are the props and baulks of timber left to shore them up. Water and general decay due to the passage of time wreak great havoc on the equipment of long ago. Do not ride on old trucks and bogeys left underground (assuming the wheels are not rusted solid) as you may not be able to stop them and you may not always know where they are going. Often they run on to some drop where their original contents were tipped out as mine debris – and you may follow the same route. Digging in mines in blocked passages may produce the same thrills of discovery to the mine archaeologist but it needs every care. I spent an intriguing time with Peter Jackson and his father in their mine explorations at Nent Head and saw just how much waste and loose material may fall down whilst digging for a way into an old section.

Mines and caves may sometimes be contaminated with sewage inflowing from outside sources and the risks from contamination from this source are not always considered. There have been recorded instances of it causing illness following contact with it in some Derbyshire mines. Some mines are inhabited by rats – and a few caves too – and they can produce a nasty form of infection known as Weil's disease. This is an infectious form of jaundice which occasionally affects sewer workers and is known to be transmitted in the urine of rats. I think there has only been one isolated case of this in a British cave picked up in Stoke Lane Slocker a few years ago. The infection could have come in from outside as the village of Stoke Lane is quite close. Luckily, the victim, a Bristol University lecturer in pathology, was able to make a swift diagnosis of his condition and extremely feverish state and obtained prompt treatment. Consequently, after the descent of a mine or cave where there is the slightest suspicion of sewage or rat contamination (some caves are also made insanitary by cavers themselves), it is wise to be extremely scrupulous in cleaning oneself afterwards, treating any cuts or abrasions with antiseptic and to seek immediate medical attention in the event of fever or internal troubles.

Another problem likely to be met with in mines are pockets of carbon dioxide, which is odourless. It can be fatal. The only time I came across it in Derbyshire, I felt some of the early symptoms of headache, nausea and a general debility. Its presence was thus suspected and the party I was with was able to get away quickly into a fresh air stream which brought about a speedy recovery. The gas may be found after excavating passages long-sealed off and these are best left alone until some ventilation is achieved.

50 One of the dangers in old mines – collapsed roof timbers as in Derbyshire.

It will be a long time before a beginner is entrusted with route finding or exploratory work. On the first descents into caves and potholes, all attention is focussed on techniques and getting used to the un-familiar underground scene. It takes time and ex-perience for a caver to learn his way around the underground world, to recognise the signs, landmarks and all the other indications of the way his route should go. On many caving trips, of course, it is possible to study in advance the geography from guide books and surveys in the various caving publications. The known and well-explored caves have well-defined routes. At first, in the general darkness, all caves tend to look the same. In time, a beginner will recognise certain things – where to look for a high passage which may by-pass a sump or impossible squeeze. The various formations may all look alike at first but they soon assume an individuality and become the signposts and markers of journeys underground. Whether one always agrees with the many and varied titles bestowed on the various formations by imaginative minds is another matter.

The requirements of route-finding and passing on

information for others to follow leads to the creation of maps of the underworld. As I have said, some cavers are jealous of their finds and guard them closely but I believe in the free dissemination of information amongst recognised and competent clubs. Admittedly, there are fools who go underground, who commit damage, despoil caves by taking out souvenirs or besmirch the landscape with their rubbish and foul habits. But, by and large, the serious-minded cavers are in the majority and have a true respect of the underworld scene and the work of others.

Cave surveying is, in fact, one of the most difficult and yet rewarding aspects of speleology. There is a growing body of competent cave surveyors in this country who have become world authorities. The work of the cave surveyor is vital in many ways – to give others knowledge, to further exploration, to make records for posterity and to relate the underworld to the world outside. The final representations may show a cave in section, in profile and by exploded diagrams relating the system to the surrounding countryside. In this country the accepted standards are laid down by the British Cave Research Association who have produced the definitive work on cave surveys by Bryan Ellis and a team of brilliant co-workers. Since the days when I was a humble tape-holder for the late Les Salmon, whose survey of Giant's Hole in Derbyshire is still regarded as something of a classic, great strides have been made in perfecting or extending various techniques. At the simplest level, a caver may just rely on his memory and a quick on-site sketch. But for the really professional product, the higher standards of survey require specialist equipment such as the theodolite, clinometer, compasses, tapes (nowadays of plastic which is durable) or the Topofil distance measurer developed in Canada which makes it simple for one man to do a lot of work.

Surveying is fascinating, for apart from the time spent on measurements of angles, dips and distances, it gives a full opportunity to study the shape and configuration of a cave and every minute detail of its make-up. It requires infinite patience and is usually undertaken on trips specially planned for the purpose. Even though you may not have the academic and scientific skills to be a competent surveyor, there is a lot to be said for helping and later taking pride in the finished map. At any rate, you should keep a notebook of your own in which to log your own cave journeys, illustrated by sketches, measurements and other details which will be of value to your own and other people's explorations. These will be of more value if you learn the various symbols in use in cave surveying both in order to understand the surveys of others and to delineate your own. My own log books and curious squiggles involving over thirty years of caving still bring back memories.

Mention of 'digs' has nothing to do with boarding house accommodation – it is short for referring to digging for new caves. It is in this direction that true

exploration still lies, either inside a known cave or outside. A small depression or hollow in the surface of an area of limestone may lead to immense possibilities underground. A slight draught from an apparently solid wall or blocked-off passageway may, with digging and probing, reveal a new part of a system and magnificent prospects of previously unseen formations and other delights of the true explorer. Hardly a week goes by without news of some new find which has rewarded many hours of patient hard work. On my heart, when I die, I am sure they will find the phrase 'Snelslow must go.' It has been the scene of much activity over the years in Derbyshire near to the Giant's Hole complex and associated swallets and caves. My friends and I have spent many hours digging, dragging out cave mud on our own little railway line, damming the in-flooding stream and blasting to make the cave wider. Nature has been winning all the time by bringing back in flood all the material which was laboriously moved.

Blasting, or 'banging' as it is more generally known among cavers, is another activity which should never be indulged in by beginners. The use of explosives underground is for experts only – and even they can come unstuck due to misfortune or foolhardiness. There is now a much more stringent control over the availability of explosives due to the activities of terrorists. Gone are the days when a friendly quarry man would hand over a mysterious – and dangerous package – for a couple of pints of beer. And I am afraid that one of my own experiences of banging probably soured the attitude of a farmer towards cavers for all time. The farm, in fact, had been vacant for some time, and my friend and I were not to know that on the day of our particular blasting, the new owner was proudly surveying his land. As he passed along this particular valley, there was a bang and a sizeable piece of Derbyshire whistled by his head from the narrow cave entrance we had been working in. It took him a long time to calm down but he was eventually placated when I showed him photographs of how this valley could flood and what we were doing would probably save the lives of his sheep by getting the flood waters away quickly.

Cavers using explosives have responsibilities, not only to themselves, but to other cavers and landowners as well. Damage to a cave environment should be avoided at all costs and should be the prime consideration in deciding whether to blast or not. The shock of a blast can have dangerous repercussions in the form of loosening rocks around the area of blasting, and fractures which are not immediately apparent may become a hazard later. Even handling explosives without protection for the hands can cause unpleasant illnesses. The fumes or gases plus dust from an explosion can prove fatal. Up to almost the end of 1979 there had been no fatalities in caving from the respiration of gases, or the absorption through the skin of nitro-glycerine. There was a serious incident in 1960

51 **Because of the number of fatalities and accidents, the Territorial Army blasted part of the mines at Alderley Edge, Cheshire, in 1957.** *News Chronicle, Manchester*

near Arncliffe in Littondale, hoping to blast their way into a new section and realise their hopes of a significant new find. They had made previous attempts to break through using smallish charges of up to 12 lb ($5\frac{1}{2}$ kg). Most of the toxic effects of proprietary explosives are known and the manufacturers give adequate warning of the hazards. Unfortunately, these two eager members of the White Rose Club of Yorkshire had prepared their own explosive mixture – one not unknown in Northern Ireland – a compound of fertiliser and fuel oil. Experts say that this should never be used underground, under no circumstances in confined spaces. Wisely, they made their detonation from the surface but, unwisely, they broke with well-established practice and went in too soon after the explosion. It is difficult to say precisely just how long a safe period should elapse before re-entry. Manufacturers and professional users fix what they believe are safe timescales. In some caves, there is adequate passage of air and safe ventilation may occur within a day or so. But some caves have static atmospheres and the fumes tend to linger. In the case of Marvel and Staniforth, they returned after only a couple of hours or so. Nor had they taken the precaution of leaving someone on the surface to give timely warning to a rescue team. The two men died from carbon monoxide poisoning from the fumes of the 30 lb ($13\frac{1}{2}$ kg) of do-it-yourself explosive.

Although they must regret the number of times they have to sit on such matters, coroners in caving areas are usually well disposed to cave exploration. And, in pointing out that permission should be sought from landowners before such blasting, the coroner Mr Miles Coverdale at the inquest in December 1979 commented: 'I don't want it to seem that I am knocking caving. It is one of the few adventure challenges, outside space exploration, left for young men. If the rules were adhered to, I would openly encourage it.' Clearly, the temptation to hurry back to check the outcome of a 'bang' must be resisted. Other cavers should also be warned that blasting is taking place and told of the date and time of any previous attempts.

Much of this kind of work, if not all, should only be undertaken with the permission of the landowner and agreement should be obtained if blasting or something in the nature of civil-engineering work is required. It is also good caving manners to respect the digs and pioneering work of others. Personally, I do not mind who follows in and carries on a dig which I have started. There may be a certain amount of glory in a breakthrough but I feel cavers should rise above such possessiveness. To share the joys of discovery, the new revelations of the wonders of Britain underground is, I believe, one of the purposes of organised and responsible speleology. Nevertheless, I agree that there should be some protection from certain elements – cowboy cavers – who infest some caving areas and who do much to damage the image of the sport in rural communities and bring speleology into disrepute.

when a thirty-five year old caver became seriously ill after detonating a charge of plaster gelatine explosive in Ogof Ffynnon Ddu. It was apparent that he had returned to the area of the explosion too soon and had inhaled a considerable quantity of fumes probably due to inhaling deeply following free-diving through a sump to check the results on the blast.

A tragic point to the dangers of returning too soon came in October 1979 with the news of the deaths of two cavers as the result of banging. Constable Richard Marvel aged twenty-five and his friend John Staniforth were expert cavers and also experienced in the use of explosives. Marvel had a certificate for the use of explosives and had taken a training course in their use. On a weekend in October they went to Cote Gill Pot

7
CAVE DIVING

Cave diving is, without doubt, the most dangerous and probably the most rewarding aspect of caving. Within limits, all dry caves are accessible to the normally equipped caver but the ultimate in exploration lies in those depths which are completely submerged. Water, the sculptural force in most limestone caves, was often the barrier to exploration even in the simplest and shortest of sumps. 'What lies on the other side?' was a question which was not answered until well into our present century.

The advice of Henry Mayhew in *Punch* magazine in 1845 to those about to marry – 'Don't' – is equally applicable to those who want to take up cave diving. It demands the highest mental and physical discipline because of the hazards and, at times, almost complete self-dependence. It is simply not enough to be a competent underwater swimmer or snorkel diver for, even with the most modern equipment, emergencies arise in cave waters which are special to their locale.

Today's modern equipment, of course, bears little resemblance to the primitive tackle first used so long ago when air was pumped manually to a diver. Little was known then of the effects of water pressure, the complications of decompression arising from too rapid an ascent from considerable depths and other physiological problems. That brilliant cave diver and poet of the depths, my friend Mike Boon, now flourishing in Canada, laconically described cave diving as 'bloody hazardous, by a factor of many', and he should know. The first recorded dive with equipment – the diver being Ottonelli of Marseille backed up by the engineer Maurius Bouvier – was on 27 March 1878 in the Fontaine-de-Vaucluse. Air was pumped to the brave Ottonelli and he got down about 75 feet (23 metres) before being forced to give up the attempt; it was sixty years before another attempt was made at the same spot.

In caving, it has always been known that diving, in one form or another, was the only way to solve some of the ultimate cave problems of this century. Exploration ceased where rock and water met at a sump. Early explorers were forced to stop at such obstacles but there were some, the foolhardy and the brave (they exist even today!) who forced themselves to the limits of human endurance to get through on sheer lung

power alone. The first lung-power dive in Britain seems to have been undertaken by an anonymous adventurer mentioned in William Bray's written account of his historical tour of Derbyshire; possibly inspired by stronger waters than those from the local springs, he tried to swim through the 'River Styx' at the Buxton Water rising in Peak Cavern, Castleton. His dive into the sump came to an abrupt end when he banged his head on a rock and sank senseless to the bottom. He was rescued alive, with difficulty. This sump did not give up its secrets until 1949 when the Derbyshire section of the Cave Diving Group, using adapted wartime frogmen's suits, got through a totally submerged passage to arrive at a 'Torricellian chamber' (in effect an airbell or vacuum completely sealed off in the rock by the surrounding water). Derbyshire still holds an important place in British cave diving.

The first great breakthrough in cave diving, which showed what could be done on lung power alone, coupled with courage, confidence and superb training, was Norbert Casteret's penetration of the Montespan Grotto in the Haute-Garonne in August 1922. When I met him on a rare visit to Britain a few years ago, he told me it was one of the hardest things he had ever undertaken but he was sustained by a firm conviction that, though *très difficile*, he would get through. In his own words, he decided to 'dare the underground river and push into the bowels of the mountain.' He made the dive naked, carrying his matches and candles wrapped in his rubber diving helmet, to keep them dry. He dived into the siphon and pressed on. Even he, with his vast experience and psychological balance, became aware of the oppressive loneliness and isolation of his position, aware that staying alive depended on keeping his few matches dry. A year later, he and Henri Godin, in slightly drier conditions, were able to proceed further to discover what many cave divers dream about, a huge treasure house of rock engravings, clay statues and other prehistoric remains. This dive encouraged others to re-think about the psychological barriers to their own explorations and more determined efforts were made to get through hitherto hopeless sumps. The alternative method of getting through was to pump or bail these siphons dry or, where possible, build dams and divert the waters elsewhere to clear an air space.

52 Hard graft – pumping to clear an air space.

outstanding in this country was Bob Leakey's dive, naked *à la Casteret* in Disappointment Pot in January 1944. This added considerable knowledge about the Gaping Gill system, solving the problem of where the waterfall came from at the end of Hensler's Passage and completing the circuit between Disappointment Pot and Gaping Gill Main Chamber. But cavers have always been inventive and several, who formed the first cave diving groups, struggled to find ways of overcoming the sump problem, tantalised by the knowledge that once through the water trap, there were great areas of potential exploration. F. Grahame Balcombe and his friend Jack Sheppard, both members of the Northern Cave and Fell Club, could be said to be the founding fathers of British cave diving. Although northerners who first became interested in the Pennine systems, they became fascinated with the caves and potholes of the Mendip Hills and the birthplace of British cave diving was the famous Swildon's Hole. The first sump (it was obviously the only one at the time) was a frustrating block to the determined efforts of Mendip cavers. In February 1934 Balcombe and Sheppard and a few others planned a campaign. Preliminary blasting had proved abortive and some way of diving had to be found. A senior engineer with the Post Office at that time, Balcombe was of an inventive turn of mind as well as a dedicated caver. He devised a diving kit which seemed inspired by the absurd ingenuity of Heath Robinson. It involved part of a bicycle frame, two valves for the intake and outlet of air, which was supplied through a 40 foot (12 metre) length of garden hose and conventional swimming goggles. It was with some trepidation that Balcombe took the first plunge and almost immediately became involved in what has always been an inhibiting factor in many water passages, the loss of visibility due to churned up mud. He was completely unnerved when he found he could not see and retreated. Sheppard fared no better. The hosepipe air line fell off as he was submerged in the passage and he got back to safety only with difficulty.

Although these two small dives were unsuccessful, sufficient was learnt to encourage further attempts with improved equipment. Further blasting, some of which is said to have elevated a Sunday congregation in Priddy church from their seats, did not improve matters and diving was resorted to, once again, in October 1936. This time Sheppard had a new outfit which provided some protection from the water, and the air came to him from a new, light-weight pump. By synchronising his breathing with that of the pumping, he ventured into the unknown and succeeded in getting through the siphon. He found, as other equipment divers have later revealed, that the intimidating sumps could be dived free, which Balcombe subsequently did. The way was known to be safe for a short, sharp dive. For a long time it was accepted as gospel truth that the 2 foot (60 cm) high passage was 10 feet (3 metres) long. But over thirty years later a more

All early attempts at diving with equipment to sustain life were handicapped by the cumbersome nature of the equipment and the problems of maintaining the supply of air. As far back as the 1860s, the French engineers Rouquayrol and Denarouze produced a regulator which allowed air to be breathed under water. Their Aerophore was a strange contraption from which the diver drew air from a heavy cylinder but, as there was no means in those days of applying compression, the supply to the cylinder had to be kept constant by an air line. The system was abandoned but the theory made a dramatic re-emergence eighty years later. The traditional diving gear was a thick rubber suit in which it was difficult to manoeuvre, a copper helmet clamped to it and to which air was pumped, and lead weighted boots which further restricted mobility. Cave diving in such equipment was almost out of the question and such dives as were made could only be in wide, open passages.

Courageous free-divers, using lung power alone, made heroic efforts to extend cave limits. One of the most scientific measurement was made by the simple expedient of passing a tape measure through the passage and the obstacle which so daunted the explorers was found to be (according to the records of the University of Bristol Spelaeological Group) a mere 34 inches (86 cm). Time and nature may have changed the length of the sump in the intervening years and, in mentioning it, it is by no means my intention to belittle this plunge into the unknown. The people who dived Swildon's were the forerunners of that elite band who now form our national body, The Cave Diving Group, founded in 1946. Cave diving received considerable impetus and encouragement from the kindly and professional interest of Sir Robert Davies of the famous diving and engineering safety firm of Siebe, Gorman & Co. who was delighted with the honour of being the CDG's first honorary president. With his support and improved equipment, attention was turned to Wookey Hole and the underground passage of the river Axe which emerges in what is known as 'Britain's oldest stately home', insofar as it provided shelter for our early forefathers.

Apart from the assistance from improved equipment, Wookey had the advantage of mainly clear water, unsullied by the thick brown mud usually found. In one of the most lyrical of caving descriptions, Penelope Powell, one of our first woman cavers and probably the first woman cave diver wrote: '. . . slipping down from the enveloping brown atmosphere, we suddenly entered an utterly different world, a world of green, where the water was clear as crystal. Imagine a green jelly, where even the shadows cast by the pale green boulders are green but of deeper hue; as we advanced, light green mud rose knee-high and fell softly and gently into the profound greenness behind. So still, so silent, unmarked by the foot of man since the river came into being, awe-inspiring though not terrifying, it was like being in some mighty and invisible presence, whose only indication was this saturating greenness.' Meanwhile, about the same time, interest was growing in underwater swimming and the largely unexplored world under the sea.

In the years before the last war, swimmers began to fix fins or flippers to their feet, while goggles and face masks allowed brief but clear glimpses of the sub-aqua world. The now legendary Jacques Cousteau was at the beginning of his long love affair with the depths and resented the restrictions imposed by pumped-air systems. About the time of the Swildon's Hole dive, Commander Le Prieur of the French navy designed a self-contained diving kit using compressed air in a portable cylinder and a face mask. Cousteau experimented with hand-pumped air lines and an oxygen re-breathing set which he had worked on with Frederic Dumas. The air line had its inherent limitations on distance and mobility and the oxygen set nearly proved fatal.

The demands of war led to many developments in underwater movement. Dunlops and their special projects general manager Wally Graham evolved the skin-tight, dry diving suit at the instigation of Major 'Blondie' Hasler of the Combined Operations Development Centre. Hasler's exploits with his canoe team in raids on enemy shipping are well known. As this type of warfare advanced, Hasler became dissatisfied with the method of attaching limpet mines to enemy ships by means of long poles. He said his men could do a better job if they could get right under the ships and this required a light and flexible skin suit. It is a remarkable tribute to Graham that the original design has changed little in the past thirty years apart from the switch to the new synthetic rubber materials like neoprene.

As cave diving resumed after the war, divers first used the old closed-circuit re-breathing equipment in which, it was found, the disadvantages outweighed the advantages of its use. In use, it required oxygen cylinders – or bottles as they are now known – a breathing bag on the chest and the use of soda lime to absorb the exhaled carbon dioxide. The greatest disadvantage in the use of oxygen is the poisoning it engenders in the blood and the brain. I will refer to this later.

Another spin-off from the war was the manufacture of more easily portable cylinders in the 1940s but the problem still remained of how to control the oxygen or air supply to the submerged diver. Commander Le Prieur's free-diving kit released a continuous flow of air which needed to be regulated to suit the diver's intake. But it was wasteful, as the air was coming out all the time. The answer lay in what is now known as the demand valve which simply provides air when the diver inhales and shuts off during exhalation. Still working on this problem, Cousteau met the engineer Emile Gagnan who had been devising gas regulators with a form of cut out, some of which were used in the wartime taxis operating on coal gas. After many frustrations the two men developed the demand valve which exactly met the diver's requirements, needing the minimum effort to fill the lungs. The valve, with the new cylinders, gave divers a new freedom from the umbilical air tube. Cousteau and Gagnan thus became the creators of a new name, the aqualung which, like some other well known trade names has passed into accepted usage. Sub-aqua diving became a new form of science and adventure revealing long-hidden secrets of the underwater world in oceans, lakes, rivers and even ponds. Once proved, the aqualung principle gravitated naturally to cavers who now had a powerful new weapon in their armoury of exploration equipment. Mention of 'weapon', incidentally, is a reminder that the first sub-aqua divers were really *nageurs de combat* (fighting underwater swimmers) but the term *homme grenouille* (frogman) captured the imagination and the name stuck.

Historically, a most significant date on which the new

systems and techniques were used in a cave environment was 27 August 1946. Once again it was at the Fontaine-de-Vaucluse where in 1878, as I have mentioned, Maurius Bouvier, Chief Engineer of the Highways Department of that region, had tried to unravel the mystery of the spring welling out from the depths. One other recorded attempt had been made, on 27 September 1938, by another Marseille diver, Negri. With much better equipment, Negri claimed to have penetrated much deeper than Ottonelli nearly sixty years earlier and said he had reached the bend in the rock where it started to rise on the other side – which was somewhat at variance with what was later discovered. In 1946, Cousteau, who was still a naval officer, and the French Undersea Research Group used the aqualung, I think for the first time in caving. He and Frederic Dumas followed the guide line already weighted into position and reached a depth of about 150 feet (46 metres) as recorded by their gauges. Unfortunately, they became affected by all the symptoms of nitrogen narcosis which may not be immediately fatal but can have disastrous consequences with its many manifestations of apparent drunkenness – disorientation, a breakdown in rationality and other forms of mental disintegration. Both Cousteau and Dumas thought the other was in danger and reached safety only with considerable difficulty. Two other officers, Taillez and Moriandière, made a second dive and a similar thing happened when they got down to about 250 feet (76 metres). It was not beyond the bounds of possibility that even with their experience and capabilities they should have succumbed to the so-called 'rapture of the depths'. It was found subsequently that they had been suffering from carbon monoxide poisoning. This is possibly the first instance of this dangerous gas being sucked into the inlet of the cylinder which was charged from the exhaust of the internal combustion engine driving the compressor. This hazard is now well known in diving circles and is guarded against. There have been many other attempts to solve the mystery of the spring at Vaucluse both by diving and investigation of the limestone plateau above it. At the time of writing, a promising new line of inquiry had to be abandoned because of a now all too familiar problem in Britain and Europe, a dispute between cavers and a landowner.

In Britain, cave diving resumed towards the end of the war, significantly at Keld Head which was later to produce a glorious page in the history of this form of diving. Grahame Balcombe returned to the fray underground with slightly better equipment but still using the oxygen re-breathing equipment then in use in the navy. He survived a number of adventures and narrow escapes involving mechanical failure and the extremely dangerous carbon dioxide poisoning. This latter could have occurred from a malfunctioning of the soda-lime purifying unit. Navigation and contact with any support team was undertaken with the Aflolaun (Aflo for short) – an acronym for Apparatus

for Laying Out Line and Underwater Navigation. This was a semi-buoyant unit carrying lights (car headlamps were favoured), a reel bearing line, sometimes doubling up as a phone link, a depth gauge and compass. Other refinements included a waterproof watch, pad for notes and messages, thermometer and any other gadgets the innovator thought essential for navigation, surveying and safety. But in the constrictions of British cave passages it was an unwieldy piece of apparatus. A far cry also from remote-controlled television robot, the Telenaut, which has also been used in the Fontaine-de-Vaucluse to a depth of nearly 350 feet (106 metres).

At first the national Cave Diving Group, formed after some notable dives in Ogof Ffynnon Ddu, at Easter 1946, favoured the use of oxygen as against the compressed air bottles becoming popular in Europe. The smaller oxygen bottles were certainly more suitable to the more constricted water passages of British caves which were mostly horizontal and shallower than the deeper sumps and springs of Europe, with the possible exception of Wookey Hole, where oxygen could not be used because of the depth-inhibiting factor. It is however, ironic, that the gas essential to most forms of life on this planet can also be dangerous, toxic in fact, and requires a professional standard of handling. So much so that its use has been banned by the country's leading diving body, the British Sub-Aqua Club.

The Cave Diving Group discontinued the use of oxygen in 1963 partly due to the greater availability of compressed air and to the success which Mike Boon had a year earlier in Swildon's. He was able to demonstrate a relatively greater freedom of movement by pushing his air cylinder ahead of him in the confines of sumps numbers six and seven. Oxygen, of course, reduces the depth limit of a dive in relation to its concentration – at 100 per cent, or pure, the Royal Navy fixes a limit of a little over 26 feet (8 metres), beyond which the risks of unconsciousness, convulsions due to the effect on the brain and drowning as a result are ever present. An oxygen-nitrogen mixture has been suggested, and used, as it increases the depth range, established by Dalton's Law of Partial Pressures, at which physiological changes ensue. This mixture, in varying proportions, was used successfully by Martyn Farr and Dave Morris in 1977 in their classic dive in Wookey Hole beyond Chamber 25. The depth at which they operated also caused problems necessitating three decompression stops which are rare in a British water passage, but then Wookey has some extremely deep water. The oxygen was to lessen the absorption of nitrogen into the body and it seemed to work.

A helium mixture has also been used but rarely, and perhaps the greatest vindication and justification for compressed air was the record-breaking dive in January 1979 by the two divers, Oliver 'Bear' Statham and

53 **Dr Ken Pearce diving at Keld Head attached to a lifeline.**

Geoff Yeadon, in their through trip from Kingsdale Master Cave to Keld Head, a distance of 6000 feet (1829 metres), the ultimate in British cave dives. Keld Head was a challenge to British cavers since the early 1920s when the possibilities of the deep pool flush to the roof of the rock, close to the narrow Ingleton-Dent road, were investigated. Pioneer of the early probes into this submerged passageway was the GOM of Yorkshire caving and rescue organiser, Reg Hainsworth. He suspected that it had intriguing possibilities and courageously made exploratory dives on ALP (Available Lung Power) with other members of the Gritstone Club. A tremendous amount of water seeps through the gaunt limestone of Gragareth which is pitted with pots and honeycombed with cave passages,

much of it emerging in Kingsdale Beck. Keld Head was nearly always full – even in times of drought – and defied all the traditional methods to lower the water to create an air space. But there was no doubt that it was connected to the intertwining passages under the fell to the west. Desultory digging and a spot of blasting failed to provide a sufficient drop in water level to enable further penetration beyond the cave mouth. Little was achieved after Grahame Balcombe's dives there with oxygen in 1944 and 1945 explored a mere 180 feet (55 metres). Forty years after Hainsworth's first efforts, a breakthrough was made by Mike Wooding, the Settle diver who made headway to a distance of over 1000 feet (305 metres) in one of the first really long British cave dives. Mike Wooding saw sufficient for him to deduce that much more lay beyond.

Further exploration in the same year of 1970, however, received a great setback by the tragic death of Alan Erith, an experienced caver but a novice diver, in Keld Head. From all accounts, he had no previous cave diving experience, and like so many in various other hazardous activities, whose eagerness and courage is not backed by training and experience, he paid the terrible penalty. Relying on what he knew of Wooding's dives, he made a preliminary dive, in the course of which he lost contact with Wooding's original guide line. He returned to the entrance with great difficulty and was considerably shaken by the experience. But, in the presence of friends, this twenty-four year old student must have been loth to abandon the enterprise. Instead of withdrawing, he had one more try, and it was all over within half an hour. The watchers gathered round the pool saw, or felt, the line jerking spasmodically and then, ominously, it stopped. A rescue team was swiftly on hand and the very experienced Wooding soon dived along the now familiar passage. He failed to find Erith, only the guide line which was cut. At the subsequent inquest, *sans cadaver*, it was surmised that he had become entangled in the guide line and struggled to cut himself free. It was possible that he had detached his mouthpiece and quickly drowned or, in his panic, lost his way and could find no way back, the end coming when his air supply gave out. Some credence was given to this latter theory when, four years later, Derek Crossland found a body 480 feet (146 metres) inside the system. It had either drifted into an unexplored side passage after death, or Erith may have swum that way thinking it was the way out. At that time Yeadon and Statham joined in the melancholy task of retrieval. It did not deter them from resuming the attack on the system both from Kingsdale Master Cave and Keld Head where I later filmed an attempt by Dr Ken Pearce and Mike Boon. Although seemingly going upstream, Keld Head was always the easier to tackle as there was the easy access from the road in this bare, atmospheric part of the limestone Pennines. A fairly routine caving trip is necessary to get into the Master Cave itself.

The through passage from darkness back into daylight has been likened to the caving equivalent of the first ascent of the North Face of the Eiger. The complete transit through the suspected continuous underwater passage created the same obsessional interest that the great Alpine climb had evoked. The siege by Statham and Yeadon went on relentlessly throughout 1976, both making dives of about 2350 feet (716 metres) from each end. In August of that year Statham established a record for Britain's longest cave dive when he plunged 2750 feet (838 metres) along from Keld Head. In Europe, the master cave diver was Jochen Hasenmayer from Stuttgart who had made a dive of 3080 feet (940 metres) and had his sights set on the first 1000 metre dive. Not to be outdone, Yeadon equalled the

German's European record in the black waters meandering under the boundaries of three counties. Then, in January 1978 Hasenmayer came to Britain to join the two Yorkshire divers, creating what was probably the most formidable European team ever to make a combined dive. It came very close to disaster. Less acquainted with the mysteries of the system, Hasenmayer missed his way and, for a tense fifteen minutes or so, seemed to be stuck with a diminishing air supply as he struggled to get through an impassable, narrow fissure. Yeadon, who went in search of the missing German, found him in conditions of almost total muddy darkness, through which his light would not pierce. It was almost by chance that Yeadon's hand touched that of Hasenmayer and he was able to use the guide line to put him on the right course round the impasse. Not given to exaggeration, Yeadon said afterwards that he believed he was shaking hands with a dead man and this part of the link in the constriction was given the macabre name of Dead Man's Handshake. Even so, the German had pressed on for 3300 feet, five metres beyond the 1000 metre mark. Six months later, Hasenmayer joined up again with the daring British pair in yet another bid to make the full, through trip. It was Statham, this time, who made the greatest progress, swimming to 3600 feet (1097 metres), returning when he knew he had only sufficient air to make the return safely to Keld Head.

The realisation of the dream of the first through passage became a certainty when Yeadon made even further progress and had the thrill of finding the guide line he had put in position only a fortnight previously, from the opposite end in the Master Cave. With that knowledge, the through trip was technically possible, but to achieve it meant mounting one of the hardest dives ever undertaken and which called for nerve, strength and a tremendous psychological balance. All that Yeadon and Statham knew, as they made their final preparations towards the end of 1978, was that there was a connection, but to cast themselves adrift hundreds of feet below the dour limestone, on the longest cave dive known to man, required superb organisation and tremendous mental discipline. The dive was also destined to become one of the most gripping real-life epics ever to be shown on television, as Yorkshire TV, with my friend Barry Cockcroft as producer, made a film of the attempt. Both for filming as well as for giving some tenuous support from above, one of the biggest problems to overcome was that of maintaining contact between the divers and the surface party. Communication underground has always presented problems – under water underground, more so. A telephone wire linkage was out of the question; yet it was vital that their progress should be checked with help, however remote at hand, in the event of an emergency. This was to be brilliantly solved by Bob Mackin of Lancaster University and a member of the Viking Caving Club of Preston. He worked unceasingly to perfect his Speleophone which is able to transmit through solid rock on a two-way basis. Through the Speleophone, conversation was possible with the divers and the anxious surface party was able to keep track on their journey.

In bitterly cold conditions and clinging mist, the above-ground party traversed the partially snow-covered upland as the divers slowly eased their way through the tight passages towards Keld Head. Flashing road-warning beacons laid out on the fell added to the eeriness of the scene as their amber lights pierced the mist. The two divers depended for their lives on the two side-carried 140 cubic foot capacity cylinders (4 cubic metres) which each of them had. They were also further burdened with extra equipment, including powerful lights for filming, a small cine-camera and tape recorder. As it was winter, and the moors thoroughly saturated the seepage from the water-logged peat hags added to the difficulties of visibility, giving the icy water an ochrous opacity. Despite the Speleophone link, Statham and Yeadon were probably the loneliest two men in Britain at that time. Part of the way through and beyond Dead Man's Handshake, they reached their cache of spare cylinders, which were essential items in their safety calculations. The planning included this necessary but well-rehearsed move to switch over to new supplies. It is not always easy to do this under ideal conditions but it was accomplished in a few tense moments to the relief of the surface party who lost some contact whilst it was being done. With the change to new cylinders and the familiar passages ahead, the divers were aware they had 'cracked it' but did not relax until they saw the first glimmerings of daylight of that chill January day. They emerged at Keld Head after what was probably the longest 150 minutes of their lives – the time it took them from the Master Cave to their debouchment at Keld Head. These two divers had triumphed over some of the worst caving conditions in Europe to establish what was believed to be the world's longest subterranean dive.

Alas, there is an extremely sad postscript to this story of incredible exploration. Only a few months after this dive and still considering the underwater challenge of other caves, Oliver Statham, in his prime at twenty-seven, took his life by gassing, ironically using the mask and breathing equipment he had used to sustain his life. He was found in his pottery workshop at Sedbergh after succumbing to chronic depression. Affectionately known as 'Bear' by all who knew him, Statham had been a caver for ten years. He had come to know and love the limestone Pennines as a schoolboy at Sedbergh and later succumbed to the lure of the depths beneath them. A dedicated and thoroughly capable caver, he grew into swift prominence and was with the British expedition which established a new depth record in the Gouffre Berger in 1972. That was the year he also started diving with his friend Geoff Yeadon and, together, they made an impressive number of discoveries in the Pennines and Mendips. He added greatly to the store of knowledge of that lonely, isolated and eerie world which is completely submerged and which few, on this planet, will ever see. In a tribute to 'Bear', Ian Plant, editor of *Craven Herald*, summed up the feelings of many when he said his countless friends were not confined to the caving fraternity. Of his cave diving, Plant wrote: 'He had an ever active, inventive mind and was a great innovator. He spearheaded many developments which advanced cave diving techniques, yet he could apply his extensive knowledge to almost any field.'

As 1979 advanced there were claims of other record dives. Two were reported in France. One was in the Vercors limestone region near Grenoble where Bertrand Leger was said to have dived 5512 feet (1680 metres) – hailed as the longest continuous dive in the world, but this is about 500 feet (152 metres) less than the Keld Head dive. The Spéléo Club de Paris also claimed to have dived 7774 feet (2400 metres) in the Trou Madame of the Limogne Plateau and to have explored another 1312 feet (400 metres) beyond the last explored sump. It will take time for these to be authenticated – records swiftly come and go – but in any event the Keld Head dive has a special place in the annals of cave exploration and will always remain as a lasting memorial to 'Bear' Statham – a great cave diver and a truly gentle man.

It is worthy of note that the rapidly developing areas of Australia have produced immensely long diving possibilities. At the time of writing Cocklebiddy Cave in the Nullabur Plain has been dived to a total distance of 10,300 feet (3090 metres).

It is inevitable that cave diving should produce a number of accidents, many of them fatal because of the reliance on equipment in circumstances when the hazards of normal caving are considerably enhanced. Diving in all its forms has special problems and the best anyone can say of any accident is that lessons will be learned which will help to eliminate such risks at a later date. This cannot always be true, of course, because there will always be people who will never learn. Dr Ken Pearce once said it was a matter of historical fact that after each cave diving death in Britain, active cave diving virtually ceased for a number of years. This is no longer completely true but each disaster has produced food for thought. In some instances, the exact cause may never be known as to why a diver succumbed. But equipment failure and/or its misuse, plus human error, are factors which cannot be ignored. The first cave diving fatality in this country happened in April 1949. James Gordon Marriott, a Manchester man and a Royal Marine Commando who became a frogman, died in Wookey Hole as he and members of the Cave Diving Group were exploring the newer chambers which were being revealed by diving exploration. He was not a member of the group and had gone along as a guest. As a frogman, he was extremely well trained and served with distinction on the D-Day landings. He had spent at least 500 hours under water. Marriott had been along to Chamber 11

54 Cave diver Dr Ken Pearce at Keld Head.

and was returning to base. Somewhere on that journey, Dr Bob Davies, a greatly experienced cave diver who was following behind Marriott, realised that somehow, in the prevailing darkness, he must have overshot the frogman. Davies and the others in the group realised that Marriott must be in dire trouble and an immediate rescue search was started. The late Donald Coase found Marriott dead, his precious oxygen being spent. It was discovered subsequently, and reported at the inquest, that a gauge which should have shown the contents of his cyclinder was inaccurate either due to incorrect setting or due to a flaw in manufacture, and he would be unaware that his oxygen was dwindling at

a lethal rate. This theory has since been discountenanced. The most significant factor was that he somehow dropped his full reserve bottle and was unable to connect himself to his vital oxygen supply.

I think it would be excessively morbid to dwell overlong on the fatalities which have occurred. Some capable and experienced people have died as well as the foolhardy and the inexperienced and one can only hope that the lessons will help save other lives. The death of Alan Clegg, for instance, was the cause of a significant change to be made in the type of demand valve authorised by the Cave Diving Group for use in underground waters. The theory was that he drowned because he lost his mouthpiece – he was using a twin-hose demand valve with back-mounted cylinders – a system prone to such an eventuality. The twin-hose system was later found to be completely unsuitable for British shallow cave dives.

The causes of death or near disaster have been many and varied. Some cave divers, notably in France, have died simply from heart attack due to stress and the cold conditions. Decompression sickness has caused several deaths. As far as I know, there has only been one fatality from this cause in this country. There is much deeper diving in Europe, in the Florida karst region where the water is often pleasantly warm, in South Africa and similar areas where the cave passages are not so constricted. External interference by others has led to a number of ordinary caving deaths and accidents where people have thrown stones down shafts or removed ropes and ladders. One young man is presumed to have died in the Porth-yr-Ogof system at Ystradfellte because, it is believed, someone untied the guide line leading back to the Top Entrance. It was certainly detached and it is thought that Paul Heinz Esser, a well-qualified diver, thought he was following it to the surface. But the unattached line led him to disaster as, travelling blind and relying on the loose line, his cylinders became empty in a flooded and unexplored part of the cave. Regrettably, some fine cavers such as Roger Solari in Agen Allwedd in south Wales in June 1974 and Mike Nelson in the Ilam risings in the Manifold Valley in the Peak District, met their deaths in circumstances still not entirely explained.

It would be impossible, in just one chapter, to produce an even theoretically capable cave diver. In the first place, it requires intense practical application in the use of a wide range of equipment and a complete understanding of the physiological aspects of surviving under water involving the body's reaction to pressure. Not all good cavers make good divers – and vice versa. Some cavers I know have an instinctive dread of water and are terrified of submergence. Usually these are the ones who have never been taught to swim and swimming is the first necessary accomplishment to acquire. Only ease in aquatic surroundings will enable a caver to overcome his fears and go right under. Even straightforward free-diving in a sump known to be short enough to do on one breath, or with air spaces for further dives, has got natural terrors for some in the claustrophobic world of unending darkness. As one of the world's leading experts on cave diving, Dr Oliver C. Lloyd, has pointed out, that 'cave diving in this country, unlike abroad, has always been for cavers who wish to dive, rather than divers who

wish to cave. It is an extension of caving and not an end in itself.' So, a member of the Cave Diving Group has got to be a good caver first. Another leading authority, Dr Ken Pearce, has recommended that the minimum requirements of a trained cave diver should be at least the attainment level of the British Sub-Aqua Club's standard for a third class diver. This requires a comprehensive knowledge of the physiological and scientific factors involved, familiarity with and the use of equipment, signals and allied matters. The correct use of the equipment, removing it, cleaning it under water, operating in complete darkness, must be practised to a degree that becomes automatic. It was such training and knowledge that saved Adrian Wilkins in Ogof Afon Hepste in south Wales. A succession of disasters led to a leak in his breathing apparatus, the loss of his face mask and another problem with his demand valve. Thanks to his training, he was able to nurse his diminishing air supply in a series of improvisations which brought him through safely.

The correct fixing of guide lines and their use as the Ariadne threads from the underworld (rarely for hauling oneself through) is also an essential part of the cave diver's art. Sometimes, finance will dictate what equipment may be used but here, as with other equipment, there are inherent dangers in second-hand or cheap equipment. Diving manufacturers generally have extremely high standards and they urge that its use should be learnt under capable supervision. The Cave Diving Group and the British Sub-Aqua Club have an immense body of expertise to give the best advice on demand valves, cylinders, harnesses, lights, signals etc., which are vital to survival in an unnatural element. Physical fitness is a prime consideration (unfortunately, epilepsy is still a disbarring disability). So is age – trainees must be above eighteen and the upper age limit is often dependent upon medical advice. The cave diving safety code lays down firm principles that a trainee diver should always be accompanied by a qualified diver until the requisite standard is attained. A solo diver should never dive without someone at base to which he should be connected by a line. And the Cave Diving Group also insists that a diver should have a 100 per cent safety margin of air for any particular dive.

I end this chapter with the cautionary words of one of the great French pioneers of diving, Michel Letrône – 'Many groups of speleologists possess or dream of possessing an aqualung but how many are prepared to wait until they are fully trained and used to moving about under water before they embark on the Great Adventure? And will they realise that unless they equip themselves with indispensable accessories, their expedition will be nothing less than suicide?'

⑧
FOOD, SURVIVAL AND EMERGENCY

It cannot be too often stressed that caving should never be undertaken light-heartedly. I am not being portentous when I say this. Cavers generally have a well-developed sense of humour as cartoons and writing in the caving journals reveal. Nor am I suggesting that caving cannot be undertaken without a sense of fun as well as a spirit of adventure. The ability to laugh makes many circumstances tolerable and relieves tension. What I am getting at is that every descent, even the apparently harmless easy caves and potholes, must be made with an awareness of the risks involved, not only to oneself but to others in the party and to rescue teams as well. It is important to know the basic means of survival in the event of an accident or the cutting off of an escape route to the surface due to flooding, roof fall or just simply by losing one's way. It has also happened that people have been left behind down a pothole which had been de-laddered simply because someone had failed to make a check list of who was with the party. It seems silly – but it happened. It meant that two families were given an unnecessary scare, an alarm was raised and the two cavers stuck down below had a long night in which to contemplate that it should be elementary to keep a tally of people's movements.

Cavers lavish care on their equipment but tend to overlook nutrition and its part in their survival. Very often, a flash-flood or sudden thunderstorm can turn the most innocuous excursion into one of survival. Water can rise below ground at a phenomenal rate and this has led to many disasters. When one is presented with this kind of emergency, food and liquid are vital factors in survival, first to maintain one's strength and energy, and also to keep up morale. No one deteriorates more quickly under conditions of stress than a cold, hungry and thirsty person.

Some cavers limit their underground nourishment to a few jam sandwiches and a flask of soup (if it survives) with little thought to the nutritional needs of the active caver or the potential deterioration due to an enforced and prolonged stay underground. Single Rope Techniques have also speeded up the former arbitrary standard times for particular trips and to some extent have reduced the amount of reliance on underground rations, but they do need to be carried. Few remember to take extra water in a clean container with them. The liquid requirements of people vary – the normal daily

requirement of a caver is between two and five pints (one to three litres) depending on body bulk. Cavers lose a lot of liquid by sweating induced by exertion in woollen clothing or the various forms of wet and dry suits. Other loss comes from the passage of urine and the exhalations of the breath. It may sound ridiculous to suggest taking water on a caving trip, especially since so much of it abounds underground. Water underground may look clean and wholesome but it is not advisable to drink such water unless in desperation. In its passage through the soil and particularly if it is run-off water in farming areas, there may be many harmful organisms in it. It is also not unknown for cavers to create their own pollution due to the inevitable requirements of bodily evacuation on the longer trips. Water purifying tablets can help to overcome this risk of a 'gyppy' stomach underground or something even worse. Carrying water from a known pure source helps to eliminate this risk as well as provide it in those dry places where there is not even a dripping stalactite to give relief. It is a good tip, on larger expeditions, to include a ration of salt in tablet form – a ten grain tablet per pint – because if the body is short of salt it cannot retain water. There is a tremendous loss of salt in sweating and it must be replaced. It is also advisable to take the salt in solution in water, since in its solid state it can cause gastric and intestinal troubles.

Dehydration can play an important part in the onset of fatigue becoming crucial over a long period without liquid so that it is a good idea to take at least a third of a pint at two-hour intervals, preferably salted, to ward off fatigue. Even if you do not feel thirsty take a drink every two hours because a feeling of thirst is not an entirely reliable indication of dehydration – the process can start without the onset of a thirst.

The food taken should not be just thrown together haphazardly but should be balanced to meet the requirements of the immense output of energy underground and also the needs of an emergency. Mr Arthur B.E. de Jong, the Development Physicist of Horlicks Limited, whose products I have used on expeditions above and below ground, and who has so kindly given me the benefit of his immense experience, suggests that a target figure of a balanced underground daily diet of 4000 kilo-calories should be aimed at. For prolonged strenuous work like laddering, crawling, digging, etc.,

5000 kilo-calories. This should be correctly proportioned as between foodstuffs containing protein, fat and carbohydrates, in addition to the minerals and vitamins. Proteins are essential for the muscle and tissue replacements, fats for energy and heat and carbohydrates to provide the balance. On shorter expeditions minerals and vitamins are not so important but on the longer stays underground they are vital. Among other things they help to combat skin disorders which occur due to a lack of sunlight, poor diet and other disabilities which occur due to the lack of opportunity for personal hygiene. Food gets used up rapidly in the body's engine on a caving trip.

Breakfast is probably the most important meal on which to start the caving day. In fact it is vital to have the inner man well fuelled before making a descent. It is not unknown for some cavers to do a fair amount of drinking on the night prior to descent and the consequent hangover affects the appetite. On anything like a serious cave expedition, it is wise to leave liquor alone for at least twenty-four hours before setting out underground. Alcohol, apart from its other vitiating effects, contributes greatly to dehydration and the onset of exposure. I know of one death from exposure in which a heavy drinking session the previous night and no breakfast the following day were the main contributory factors in the onset of a fatal coma. The person concerned just literally laid down and died because he had no reserves of energy from within to combat the rapid onset of physical deterioration. An average-sized breakfast would probably have saved his life.

Cavers invariably have healthy appetites and the breakfast which has been the start of all my climbing and caving days – porridge, bacon and eggs, beans and fried bread plus liberal lashings of tea – contains enough calories to produce a peak energy level at one and a half to two hours, from when the energy curve begins gradually to decline. Replenishing should take place, if possible, in up to two to three hours after the breakfast (or supper of equal value if it is a night descent); if the trip is to be twelve hours or over, arrangements should be made for at least one substantial cooked meal at some suitable rendezvous. Choose food which gives a good power-to-weight ratio working towards, say, 11–14 per cent protein, such as meat, eggs, fish, milk; 25–35 per cent fat (meat, butter, margarine, lard or cooking lard); and the rest in carbohydrates such as flour, cereals, bread, sugar, etc. Leaders should also insist on each member of a party carrying a small personal emergency pack which, wisely used, can sustain a reasonable degree of survival for a forty-eight hour period. Such a pack, containing two and a half ounces (70 grams) of oatmeal block, one and a half ounces (42 grams) of glucose tablets, and two ounces (57 grams) of barley sugar, carefully rationed with two pints (1 litre) of water has been devised and tested and will do the trick.

Alternatively, if the party is large and sharing loads for an extended stay, special ration packs are available containing enough energy foods for two or more days. Dehydrated or accelerated freeze dried foods (AFD), the products of modern technology, are now available. The latter just needs boiling water added to provide meals which, if not exactly *cordon bleu*, are appetising and nourishing underground. Sausage, bacon and beans – the caver's traditional meal – may be yielding to the more succulent-looking turkey tetrazinni, Mexican omelette or chicken stew, topped off with butterscotch pudding or granola and blueberries. These products of Mountain House Foods and other packs – the Norwegian SR and Verkade emergency rations – are ideal and are no great weight to carry. In some cave systems, some emergency supplies are stored for emergencies only and tests have shown that they have survived in caches in various places for several years.

One of the most frequent emergencies in caving arises from being cut off by water or being isolated from the main party by careless wandering. Survival needs concentration, common sense and the control of any feelings of panic. Being trapped by water really should not happen but it does. Throughout Britain, as elsewhere, caves which are known to flood should be avoided at the slightest risk of heavy rain. No one knows in this country when a simple rainstorm will develop into something of monsoon proportions. When it does happen the effect above and below ground is awe-inspiring.

Once, during a dig at an old mine at Snelslow in Derbyshire, one such storm swept the Peak District; if I had not got a series of photographs, some taken neck-deep in water, I still could not believe it really happened. A tiny stream runs into Snelslow which, I suspect, breaks into the Giant's Hole system and with members of my own potholing club we had built a small concrete dam at the entrance to divert the stream water into a secondary passage. We also had a sign 'Do not enter when flooded', thinking that the water rose only just above the sill of the dam. What we had not bargained for was that not only did the dam disappear under water – the complete cave entrance was submerged by a raging torrent which filled the valley well up the side of Snelslow and disappeared in a great vortex down a swallow hole beyond. It was a terrifying example of the water power which can isolate cavers and lead to such tragedies as Mossdale Cavern in Yorkshire in 1967 and the disappearance of a lone caver in Goyden Pot, Nidderdale in 1957 – the twenty-year-old Leeds art student, Brian Andrew Kerr.

There are a number of useful points to bear in mind if trapped in a cave for any reason. One may be alone or with a small group. The first and vital essential is to keep calm and evaluate the situation. If water is rising it is important to get to a place beyond the reach of the rising torrent. If one has just been thoughtlessly left behind, it is best to get to the nearest possible point of rescue. With proper leadership no one *should* be left.

Flooding creates a different situation and it could be days before a rescue team can successfully get in, depending on the weather and the strength of the rescue resources. Talking to Lewis Railton of the South Wales Caving Club of the occasion when he and Bill Little were cut off for fifty-nine hours in Ogof Ffynnon Ddu in 1951, I asked him for some of his impressions. Significantly one of the things he stressed as most important was the need to carry a reliable, waterproof watch, preferably one with a date window. The reason for this, he told me, was that without a watch there is no means of measuring time and when it comes to rationing food out this is a crucial factor. An hour seems like an age and there is a temptation to eat food at the dictates of one's stomach rather than to spread the food out at very definite intervals. As he pointed out, 'without means of recording the passage of time, three days' ration of food could be eaten in twelve hours.' If no watch is available it is a good idea to revert to one of the oldest forms of measuring time – marked candles. All cavers should carry spare candles, which have a fairly standard rate of burning providing draughts can be excluded. It should be well worth while at some club meeting to establish on a candle the rate of burning of say an hour and mark it. Then it would not be difficult to produce a number of graduated candles with snicks or black lines to give a fair idea of how time is passing.

Having reached a dry point of the cave, get off what damp clothing you can and replace it with any dry gear you have. If a towel is carried – there should be one at

55 & 56 **The power of water. 55 The start of a flash flood in the valley below Snelslow, Derbyshire. 56 Twenty minutes later and the cave entrance at right was completely submerged.**

least in a camera kit – have a brisk rub down before putting on the dry gear. Again, it is important to conserve energy, so while the emergency lasts it is advisable to sit or lie down so that little as possible of the energy-producing food and drink is consumed in wasteful physical action. Try to get warm and stay warm. If there is a draught, try and build a small shelter with stones and mud but, particularly if the cave is a confined space, do not dig a trench to lie down in, especially in sand, as this can cause a pool of exhaled breath in the form of CO_2, carbon dioxide, to build up. This in itself can start a vicious circle by speeding up the respiratory rate and adding to the physical and mental deterioration with headaches, general weakness and dizziness. It does not require any great diminution of oxygen to affect the nervous system. You are in trouble when the oxygen from the inspired air drops from the normal 21 per cent to between 16 and 12 per cent; at that moment anoxemia develops – oxygen deficiency. In such a confined space a candle or any other naked flame is a bad thing – but it can give a guide to the danger of the situation as it usually burns out at 17 per cent. Deterioration comes on in many ways. One of them is the psychological lowering of morale due to exposure and the environment. Cave malaise or sickness can be a very real thing. I would also recommend trying to find a quiet part of the cave system in which to sweat it out away from the roar and rush of water. As time goes on the unending drumming of water can get on one's nerves. It seems to numb the senses and the knowledge that it is rushing along to the outside world increases the temptation to jump in and go along with it to try and find a way out that way. Watching it continually has a hypnotic effect – although a regular watch should be kept as to whether it is rising or falling. Professor Alfred Bögli, who was trapped for ten days with four men in one of the largest cave systems in the world, the Höloch in Switzerland, said that immense mental discipline was necessary to refrain from trying to get through the flood waters. His party had gone in only for a day, unprepared for a longer stay, and their escape is a reminder of what can be achieved through not yielding to panic and eking out food supplies, however meagre.

If you do move into a deeper and drier part of the cave, leave some indication of where you have gone for the rescuers who come along. White cards in polythene covers are useful to leave around in some eye-catching spot, or an arrow made with stones, or as a last resort a message scorched on any dry part of the cave wall with a candle or carbide flame. All these of course presuppose that there is no telephone link to the outside of the cave and no stand-by surface party.

With a party there is always a temptation to separate, particularly since tempers do not improve as the strain builds up. Decide on a leader to cope with the emergency and stand by his judgement. And keep a log if you can of all the things that go on. Write down the times of food taken, when the next meal is planned; also any physical changes in the atmosphere of the cave, the time water levels rise and fall, conditions of personnel. These are disciplined acts which absorb time and help to concentrate the mind away from the situation. And if there is no danger of a CO_2 build-up, sing. One of the greatest dangers to a trapped party is psychological, and singing or chanting anything from the Rubaiyat of Omar Khayyám to Eskimo Nell can do no end of good. One thing is certain: no matter how bad things seem, a rescue team will be on its way. You owe it to them to keep as fit as possible with a good morale for when the moment comes to make the journey back to the surface. In that way you can help yourself and help them.

The increasing number of accidents underground led to the creation of cave rescue organisations. Not all of the accidents have involved genuine cavers. These incidents usually occur in easily accessible places such as the old copper mines at Alderley Edge in Cheshire. Most of them happened to foolhardy youngsters whose sole equipment was either a cycle lamp or a flash lamp who wandered in and either fell or got lost. The CROs, as they are known, first began functioning before the last war when it was realised that to retrieve an injured person from a cave, along passages and up shafts, involved the development of special equipment and methods. Today, Britain's cave rescue teams are efficient and well organised, unified in a national body, the Cave Rescue Council, which co-ordinates the eleven CROs throughout the British Isles, including Northern Ireland. Each caving area has its own rescue teams which, in the event of some major catastrophe, are available to help each other. These teams, it must be stressed, are entirely voluntary and give their services willingly to retrieve their fellows involved in accidents. In recent years, this work has been recognised, somewhat belatedly, by the Government, and the CROs get some financial assistance and insurance through the Home Office. Up to the time of writing, that insurance affects only the rescue of humans. Nonetheless, CROs have undertaken many mercy missions to retrieve farm animals, and helping the RSPCA whenever needed. The teams usually operate on a 'snowball' system with a stand-by team on duty each weekend and back-up teams called out if required. The call-outs are routed through the divisional police headquarters in each area who contact the on-duty rescue controller. The rescue teams have on hand basic rescue material such as ladders, ropes, pulleys, excavation tackle, jacks for lifting boulders, specially devised stretchers, pumping and diving gear. Medical kits are also provided and most, if not all of the teams, have a caving doctor on the strength. The teams stage regular rescue exercises to gain experience of all the equipment and make a careful study of the known hazards in the various systems in their area. Many of these hazards are well known, even notorious, attracting the foolhardy because of their notoriety. Accidents may be due to a genuine slip or mistake. More often

57 Alistair Mcdonald, BBC 'Look North' reporter, who volunteered to try out Derbyshire Cave Rescue Organisation's specially adapted stretcher.

a caver incapacitated by injury. In these so-called 'black holes' thought has had to be given to the possibility of hospitalising the victim *in situ* until he or she is fit enough to endure the rigours of the return to the surface. It is an appalling thought but, mercifully, it has not happened yet. In the last resort, should such a calamity happen, high-speed drilling through the strata would be the only possible alternative to a long and agonising wait in conditions where recovery would be low. It has been suggested that this might have saved the life of Neil Moss in Peak Cavern but the rock was too thick and the time factor was against it.

The Cave Rescue Council has evolved a simple acronym aimed at reducing the possibility of an accident – *A Plan To Be Safe*. Each letter is the key to a safety code – *A*lways include experienced cavers in the party. *P*ick a cave or pothole within everyone's capabilities. *L*eave a note of your trip and latest time of return with responsible persons and report to them on your return. *A*sk for – and act on – local advice. *N*o less than four in the party and keep together. *T*ake notice of the local weather forecast. *O*ne reliable cap lamp for each person. *B*oots, helmets and warm clothing are essential. *E*mergency lights, food and first aid kit should always be taken. *S*ee that ladders, belays and ropes are inspected and rigged properly before hanging your life (and others) on them. *A*ccident underground is always easy; rescue is sometimes difficult; sometimes impossible. *F*alls, loose boulders, rising water and exposure cause most accidents. *E*xit takes more effort than entry – plan with the return in mind.

In the event of an accident there are certain broad guidelines to follow. The leader will have to make a quick but thorough assessment of the situation, first to care for the injured person and then ensure that there is no additional risk from the same hazard i.e. falling boulders, breaking ropes, ladders etc. The casualty will need immediate attention in the way of first aid and protection from further injury. An injured caver has been known to roll off a ledge whilst others were discussing what to do about him. Correct diagnosis is a matter for the experts but people with first-aid knowledge should be able to identify fractures, bleeding of various forms and the extent of shock. Head and spine injuries call for extreme care. Once a fairly accurate identification of what is wrong has been established, two people should be sent to the surface to call the CRO. The simplest and normal way is through the 999 emergency system to the police, who will alert the rescue team. Some people might feel diffident about a call which could in the end involve scores of people – the police, fire brigade, ambulance service, the WRVS (a great help on big rescues) as well as the rescue team. Whilst most rescuers resent the occasional 'daft' turnout, they would rather be on the scene quickly to

than not they are due to inexperience, over-evaluated experience or an 'it can't happen to me' philosophy. There has also been concern that a disproportionately large number of recent accidents have occurred in school or youth parties taking part in organised activities, commendable in itself, but disastrous if incompetently led and organised. But, at the time, cave rescuers do not sit in judgment on the pros and cons of whether people should have done what they did – they get on with the job, no matter how difficult. The examination of the causes comes afterwards.

In the past few years due to extended explorations of remoter and more inaccessible parts of the underworld, it has become clear that there are over fifty caves from which it would be almost impossible to bring out

58 Cave rescue technique being demonstrated at the International Caving Congress. Specially designed stretcher and polythene sheeting in use to protect the casualty from water.

appraise the situation. In passing the message it is important that the cave or pothole should be correctly identified, as well as its location. Police do have various guide books on hand in some stations, but these are now mostly out of date and the number of sites have proliferated, many being outside the usual caving areas. Passing the correct message is all important since it may be affected by vagaries of the telephone system or mishearing. The hoary old wartime chestnut about an urgent message 'send reinforcements' being translated as 'send three and fourpence' has some basis in fact. Some cave and pothole names sound very much alike and may be in different parts of the same area. 'Oxlow' in Derbyshire sounds very much like 'Oxclose', some miles away and, on the phone is not unlike 'Knotlow', which is in a different direction altogether. 'Lord's Top Hole' in Kingsdale is not dissimilar from 'Tot Lord's Hole' in the Attermire area. The time and nature of the incident should be included in the first message, at what place in the cave system it occurred, the nature of the party and conditions in the cave.

Attempts to move the casualty by other members of the party should, meanwhile, only be undertaken on the surest grounds that no further aggravation of the condition will be caused. The victim should not be left alone, for many reasons. Psychologically he may feel he has been abandoned and the instinct for self-preservation may compel him to worsen his condition by a further accident or increased stress on the afflicted parts. Hence the need for an underground party having sufficient members to cope with this kind of situation. On arrival at the accident location, the rescue team should be completely in charge; arguments are best left until it is all over.

Apart from specific injuries, there is also the risk of the onset of hypothermia (exposure). This may occur independently of any injury and the result of deterioration due to the cold and wet environment. This causes a heat loss which becomes dangerous with the added factors of fatigue, anxiety and mental stresses, lack of food and sleep or the psychological phenomenon known as 'cave depression'. Physiologically, the body needs to maintain a central or 'core' temperature of 98.8°F (37°C). Exposure develops when the body's peripheral blood is cooled rapidly and, in circulating, reduces the inner or core temperature to a degree which affects the mind and muscle co-ordination, leading to unconsciousness and death. All leaders should be on the alert for the symptoms of exposure in the party which manifest themselves in reduced performance, lassitude, unreasonable behaviour, shivering and weakness to the point of collapse. When hypothermia is suspected, it is no use continuing with the trip and an immediate evacuation from the scene is necessary. Death can be very rapid, within a few hours, unless all precautions are taken. The afflicted should be provided with extra warm clothing, warm drinks and energy-giving foods such as glucose or sugary substances. Extra warmth may be provided by the party huddling together communicating body warmth to the victim. At all costs the temptation to apply hot water bottles, rubbing or the stimulus of alcohol must be avoided as this brings forth blood from the deeper recesses of the body where it has been maintaining inner warmth. Brought to the surface, it cools and in its circulation back to the core, it cools the core. Shivering is a sign of the body's efforts to create warmth; as the inner temperature drops it ceases, a sure sign of crisis. That is why alcohol is such a danger – it stimulates the peripheral blood vessels but does great harm because the ultimate effect is cooling to the core temperature. In a mountaineering context I once wrote 'It is a chastening thought that if the legends of the kind-hearted and well-meaning monks with their St Bernard dogs and the traditional flasks of brandy are true, they may have been the means of despatching more people than they saved – howbeit, happily.'

One way of insulating a victim is to provide a cover which will exclude further cold and damp and retain body warmth. In its simplest form a polythene plastic bag is useful. One of the spin-offs from the exploration of space has been the evolution of 'space blankets' working on the principle of high insulation. These may be of the disposable variety or of a more permanent material, depending on price. Treatment of the exposure victim, on recovery, should be under strict medical supervision and using the latest techniques.

If the rescue looks like being a long one, the controller will assemble other teams to take over as the conditions require. The great essential with the underground party is to avoid panic and to co-operate with the rescue team. Often the best way of doing this is to get outside without making things worse. Some people have survived under incredible privations underground in the face of extreme odds against their being rescued. And it is remarkable how few of the victims ever return to offer a modest 'thank you' to volunteers who have risked all in order that others might survive. Should people be made to pay for being rescued? That argument has been bouncing around the climbing and caving world for a long time. On balance I think most cave rescue teams prefer things the way they are, on a voluntary basis. The next time you see a CRO collecting box in a pub in the hills, it might be worth the thought that this is where most of the money comes from – voluntary contributions. Sad to say, but rarely from those rescued or their families.

9 PHOTOGRAPHY

'Take nothing but photographs – leave nothing but footprints.' This is the motto of the good caver who has concern for the preservation of the underground environment. Photography is an important part of caving, both in providing a permanent record of all aspects of the underworld and its contents, and is also a useful tool in the surveying and recording of caves and potholes. It takes a lot of effort to convince people that there is a wealth of colour down there to be captured by the camera as well as wonderful opportunities for studies in black and white. But photography underground poses problems of a special nature because most of the enemies to good photography exist there – water, dirt, mud, sand and a pervading atmosphere of dampness. There is also the inevitable banging, shaking and immersion in water that goes with journeys down shafts, narrow passages and crawls. To cope with all the hazards to which it is inevitably subject, the equipment – cameras, lenses, lighting arrangements – must be robust. Moreover, the equipment must have the maximum protection in transit in order to survive and do its work. And it must work for, in many cases, particularly in far flung and deep expeditions, the opportunities for re-shooting may never occur again.

The main emphasis in this chapter will be on still photography. At one time cine photography was somewhat prohibitive on the grounds of expense but there have been some fine amateur films made at reasonable cost. Obviously the first essential of photography is the camera and today there is a bewilderingly large variety from which to choose. In the end it comes down to what one can afford although some clubs or groups are able to pay more for their equipment than the individual. The two most convenient sizes of camera for cave photography are those which take films giving a format of $2\frac{1}{4} \times 2\frac{1}{4}$ inches (6×6 cm) on paper-backed film spools; and the 35 mm. The so-called half-frame cameras using half a 35 mm film frame did have a short vogue but since then a number of full-frame cameras of matching compactness have appeared to oust their smaller brethren. The half-frame cameras are nevertheless economical and on long trips where every ounce of equipment has to be carefully considered, they have the virtue of reducing the amount of film stock which needs to be carried. My personal preference is for the $2\frac{1}{4}$ inch square format for

black and white photographs which are required more for printing enlargement than projection; and the 35 mm size for colour transparencies. There are, of course, colour films, in the $2\frac{1}{4}$ inch square range and there are some projectors which will accommodate both sizes in specially adapted slide carriers.

Quite a number of 35 mm cameras are inexpensive and even some of these offer the facility of interchangeable lenses, wide angles, telephoto, close-up and extension tubes for ultra close-up work. All these add versatility to one camera but they are not all necessary, certainly not telephoto lenses. A camera tends to become a personal thing like a huntsman's gun with all its abilities, limitations and idiosyncracies becoming known. I still have a great affection for and use of an old, battered Solida 111 with bellows opening, a 2.9 lens and a Prontor S shutter with a self-taking device. The latter is extremely useful on any camera for getting into one's own pictures and vital to prove the veracity of some solo-caving exploits. The great things to avoid are falling over or accidentally kicking the tripod leg in the dash to get into position in the few seconds allowed by the timing device. The Solida has survived being blown away in a whirlwind in the Himalayas (by a freak chance a Sherpa found it on a rock, open and ready to take a picture), a fall with me attached in Nettle Pot and several immersions including a complete baptism in an underground river in Norway. Some cave photographers do not care for bellows cameras because that is the part most vulnerable to damp and holing.

Another disadvantage is that it is often difficult to see the wind-on sequence of dots and numbers in poor lighting conditions and there is nothing more frustrating than to have overlapping frames. This is avoided by cameras with wind-on mechanisms which also set the shutter. Twin-lens reflex cameras come into this category but, generally, they are too bulky for cave photography although they do make focussing and composition much easier. These also take interchangeable lenses. So do the Hasselblads and Bronicas but these range from over £500 to over £1000, too expensive to risk in caves. Whilst touching on the matter of price, I might as well mention insurance. All equipment is worth insuring but check that the policy is wide enough in scope to cover loss in caving

activities. I know of one caver who had to fight immensely hard to regain the insurance value of his camera because it was lost in 'un-normal' activities. It is arguable whether one needs a wide range of shutter speeds – they are necessary for electronic flash and for freezing the action of water or other movements. The basic requirements should include the facility for opening the shutter, usually marked B for bulb setting, or with the slow speeds of 1/25 or 1/30 of a second. In some cameras, it is not always possible to opt out of the systems provided to cope with the different aspects of cave photography and the ability to

override the automated settings or provide open flash is vital. It is a matter of personal preference whether one wants to 'freeze' running or falling water or to leave it as a streaky blur. Similarly with such actions as abseiling, swimming or other scenes of mobility, a hint of movement is often considered to be more artistically desirable. In any event, it is wise to take most pictures from a tripod to eliminate camera shake. It also goes without saying that there must be a means of attaching a flash gun and a contact point – most cameras have indications for flash bulbs e.g. X or a bulb symbol, and electronic flash e.g. M or a zig-zag arrow.

Another factor in the choice of camera is the size of the view-finder. The viewing hole on many cameras is often inadequate for the purpose of sizing up a cave scene unless it can be brilliantly lit beforehand with something like the cine operator's portable 'suns' or

59 (left) An action shot of a caver climbing a cascade in Alum Pot, Yorkshire. *Sheena Stoddard*

60 (below) Beauty in the pools of Spar Cave on the Isle of Skye. Access to the cave is dependent on the tide. *Tony Oldham*

big hand lamps carried for the purpose. One way to overcome this is to use a camera with a direct or sports view-finder – it is not difficult to make one if it is absent. Of the 35 mm cameras available, I find it almost impossible to recommend any particular one as price is often the clinching factor. The range is so wide these days – mostly German, Japanese and Russian. The budding cave photographer would do well to investigate the second-hand shops where perfectly adequate equipment is available at a reasonable price. Perhaps the ultimate caver's camera is the superb Nikonos III in the Nikon range. It is completely waterproofed without need of a special housing, which keeps weight and bulk down, but the basic body and a standard lens is close on £200 and a 28 mm wide angle will cost nearly that much, or nearly £600 for a 15 mm, 2.8 lens. Few cavers could afford such an outlay but it could be an investment as part of club equipment. Recently I have been using a much cheaper Japanese camera, the Fujica HD1 which is water-, mud- and dustproof. With its water resistant strobo flash and click focussing, it has solved many of my problems. Simplicity in one's equipment is a great asset. Unless one is a specialist in optics or hyper-critical to the nth degree, it is difficult to detect the difference in quality between lens in the cheaper 35 mm cameras and those in the high cost bracket. I have used a couple of old Exa cameras for several years, finding them extremely versatile with a wide range of accessories capable of covering all cave photographic eventualities including extension tubes for ultra close-ups. Two cameras are useful anyway for taking black and white and colour but it is wise to clearly mark which film stock is in which camera, preferably by a plastic sticker as not all cameras have film speed indicators and, if they have, they are often difficult to see.

Whilst bulk and weight must be considered, it is often worth while taking along one of the instant print cameras in situations where it may not be possible to repeat a particular shot. The Polaroid SX range and the Kodak instant camera range have now progressed so well that it is worth the extra weight to know one is certain of a picture as there are so many things to go wrong with cameras and flash. A Polaroid camera saved the day for me in Arctic Norway when my 35 mm camera failed. It is now no longer necessary to heat up the print in a metal plate under one's armpit or other warm region, often a difficult and messy process underground. But it is vital to have a clean, dry container to carry out the prints. It will be obvious that clean hands are necessary for handling such prints as well as the other equipment in use, so it is worth mentioning at this stage that rubber gloves will help to keep the hands clean and a towel in a dry container is a 'must' for drying hands, wiping off perspiration which tends to drop from the forehead on to the camera body and mopping other extraneous moisture. A tape measure is also a valuable asset for the accurate measuring of distances between the camera and the

61 The Nikonos III camera which does not need a protective housing for underwater photography.

subject, particularly with the split image range-finders which are sometimes hard to operate in low light conditions.

Having got the camera, it is essential to have something on which to stand it. At speeds below 1/25 with open flash, it is impossible to avoid camera shake (one of my photographers had such bad nerves that anything below 1/500 had movement), particularly if the photographer has been doing something energetic beforehand. Sometimes, it is possible to stand the camera on a convenient piece of rock but many cameras tend to tilt due to the weight of front mountings. Therefore a tripod is required. Apart from helping to eliminate shake, it is helpful in composing pictures and when more than one flash is being used. To withstand the battering it will get underground, a tripod must be sturdy. I do keep reiterating that weight is important. A few extra ounces may feel like pounds at the end of a hard day but I think it is worth the slight inconvenience of weight in order to get extra stability. My longest-serving tripod is too heavy for some, but it has survived many a hard knock, including a drop down Garby's shaft in the Gouffre Berger, and is still going strong. Remember always to clean your tripod, and indeed all your equipment, after each trip. Cameras should be allowed to air out in a warm, dry room and mud should be washed off tripod legs and sluiced from moving parts, preferably before the mud has had time to set hard. A light application of petroleum jelly afterwards also helps the moving parts. Some tripods have tilt and angling heads – otherwise you can buy a ball-and-socket head which gives these movements. Another advantage of the tripod is that it can be used to mount two cameras at once on extension bars, thus economising on flashes. In this way black and white and colour shots of the same scene can be taken either by using films of about the same speed rating, or compensating for any difference in speed by an adjustment of the stop. Otherwise, the adjustment may also

62 The almost tactile quality of superbly lit formations, Easter Grotto, Easegill Caves in Yorkshire. *John Forder*

be made in the processing. And an extension bar may also be used to move the direction of the light source to one side, to avoid some of the flat, frontal lighting from a flash gun fired directly from the camera shoe. This has often led to the 'red-eye' phenomena which makes human posers look like were-wolves or the victims of an extremely bad hangover. This is due to the red reflection from the retina and the choroid or pigmented area behind it, especially in low light or absolutely black conditions. It can be avoided by the subject looking away from the direct line of firing.

This brings me to the complex problem of the light source itself. Before flash bulbs, cave photography was a much more hit-or-miss affair than it is today with the use of flash powder or magnesium flares and long exposures for available light from candles, torches and headlamps. Flash powder is now rarely used, if ever. It rejoiced under the sobriquet of 'smokeless', a misnomer if ever there was one, as it often gave off a whitish fog which percolated along various passages to the chagrin of other photographers. Despite the claims of the manufacturers, it was also unstable and my frontal baldness is the result of making too close an inspection of a mound of powder in Gaping Gill when the fuse went off after all. It was perhaps best in places like the main shaft of Gaping Gill where the smoke could funnel out like the plume from a volcano. Despite all efforts, the powder would get damp and the explosive nature of its make-up has been known to damage fragile formations. Whilst it gives an extremely pretty effect, magnesium ribbon has the disadvantage of creating smoke which hinders further photography whilst leaving exposures and stop numbers in the realms of conjecture.

The choices today are between expendable flash bulbs, electronic flash units, and flash cubes. The latter may be ruled out almost immediately except for fairly close work because the reflector area is only the size of the cube giving a limited 'throw'. Electronic flash equipment which is capable of giving a number of flashes can be expensive and vulnerable to cave conditions. This equipment has the advantage of being rechargeable in some models and, after the first fairly high cost of purchase, has a low price per flash of extremely short duration – up to 1/2000 of a second – but with a colour temperature capable of accommodating black and white and colour films. Some experts consider that there is a risk element involved in electronic flash developing high voltages in the conductive damp atmosphere found in most caves and potholes. Because electronic flash has more or less swamped the market, bulb flash has taken a back seat and the variety of guns for its use has accordingly diminished. But, on balance, I think the flash bulb best for most cave photography – the bulb size is variable with a broad spectrum of light capacity which may be permutated in various ways to cope with the speed of the film stock and the situation to be photographed. A reflector is essential. Some flash guns have a useful, folding fan device which takes up little space – the old Kobuld U 1 is an example. More than one flash gun is often required in big caverns or large shafts and these may be triggered off by extra extension cables or using the open flash method – an open flash button should be part of this equipment for caving purposes. Also useful is a spring-loaded bulb ejector to save burning one's fingers when the bulb is spent (remember not to leave it lying around and take it out with you). So is a built-in test bulb which can be used to see if the circuit is working satisfactorily. This is best done before making a descent rather than make the discovery underground when there may be no chance to rectify anything that is wrong. Colour flash bulbs also have a spot indication in the safety bead to indicate deterioration and lack of effectiveness – and this again should be checked before descending.

The bulbs most frequently used underground are PF 1 or PF 5 which are capless. Some flash guns will take only this type, but there are others which take the bayonet fitting and there is an easily fixed adaptor which will enable them to take capless bulbs as well. Incidentally, a quick lick to moisten the end of the capless bulb helps to clean the end and improve the contact. Blue flash bulbs are best because they can be used with both daylight colour film and black and white. Then there are the more powerful bulbs which require screw-in sockets and have an immense light output. Multi-contacts may also be used with extension leads to provide modelling and a greater coverage with light. Then there are the so-called 'slave' units such as those made by Bowens which are triggered off by another light source, usually the flashgun on the camera but sometimes by a headlight or torch which is useful under certain circumstances. The trouble with slave adaptors which operate on their sensitivity to light is that setting them up without triggering them off with one's own lighting can be quite difficult. I have been temporarily 'blinded' more than once by carelessly turning my headlight towards the bulb in the slave unit. The best thing is to try and establish the slave in position, load the bulb in complete darkness and shield one's own lamp when returning to the camera location. Sometimes the lesser light factor of candles is useful in this regard, saving damage to the eyes as well as the expense of wasted bulbs especially if the big 'blasters' are being used.

Back to the camera and a lens hood is useful for protecting the lens from water dropping and reduces the possibility of flaring from side lighting. An optically correct glass in the filter ring also helps to provide extra protection to the lens. It prevents mud, dust and water getting to the sensitive area of the lens itself and is easy to clean and replace if damaged. A soft lens brush and lens-cleaning tissues should also be included in the kit. But direct application to the lens of even these purpose-made accessories should only be done as a last resort as fine particles of grit can ruin a lens – hence the protective glass in the lens hood. The equipment needs protection in transport underground

63 An out-of-sight, independent unit supplemented the flash gun on the camera to give a feeling of distance in Peak Cavern, Castleton, Derbyshire.

too, in order to minimise and cushion the inevitable bumps and bangs and keep out the prevailing wetness. The custom-built carrying cases for above-ground photography would not withstand the strain of underground transportation. Some cavers make their own waterproof carrying boxes but the old WD surplus ammunition boxes are probably still best. They are strong, have suitable carrying rings and can be made effectively protective with impact-absorbing foam. It is a useful tip to paint such boxes a bright red, yellow or white because the usual dun or khaki of their original state tends to merge into the mud and rock background and become difficult to find if not lost altogether. A smaller tin may be adapted with protective foam to carry flash bulbs. These may then be removed from their cardboard carton. The guide number chart may be stuck in the lid with see-through tape or a simple exposure calculator setting off stops against distance; shutter speed and distance can be devised to suit one's particular equipment. This helps to remove the problem of trying to read soggy and often mud-stained cartons, and reduces risk of adding to the unpleasant mound of cave litter found these days, however accidentally.

Plastic bags are ideal for keeping the moisture out but they do have a tendency to 'sweat' thus adding to the condensation problems; this also occurs with the floatable canoeist's carrying bags which are useful for carrying photographic gear underground. One way of combating this is to use silica gel crystals in sachets to absorb some of the moisture – the best are those with a chemical indicator warning when the gel has become saturated and is no longer working. Another moisturous bugbear of cave photography is condensation due to the transition of equipment from colder to warmer atmospheres and caves tend to be cooler than the external temperature. If time permits, it is a help to let the equipment 'acclimatise' right at the beginning of a photographic trip. The temptation to wipe 'steam' off lenses should be resisted and does little good as the internal elements are often affected as well. Condensation also comes from exhaled breath and from cavers' bodies and has been known to mar an otherwise good picture.

Photographers both above and below ground can argue for hours on the choice of film and the merits and de-merits of the different brands – Kodak, Ilford, Agfa, Fuji and a few others. At the beginning it is best to experiment a little and stick to one type of black and white and one type of colour until their full characteristics are known under all kinds of conditions, latitude in terms of exposure and performance under the various development techniques. The choice is an extremely individual one with consideration being given to the use of the ultimate result – slides for

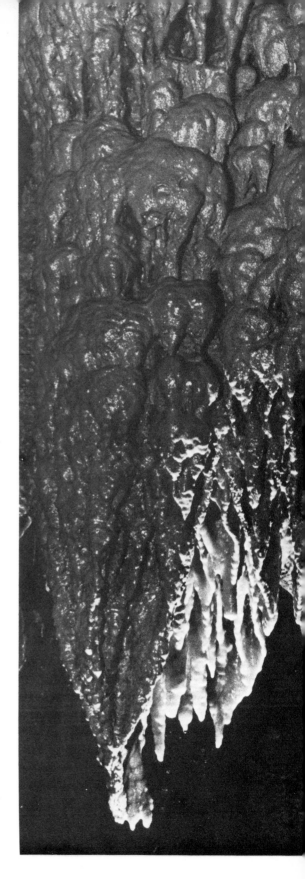

64 Travertine formations glisten in the light, Mammoth Cave National Park, USA. *National Park Service of the US Department of the Interior*

projection, negative for colour prints and black and white prints. Through trial and error I have settled for Kodak Ektachrome and Tri-X Pan, both now as fast at 400 ASA which helps standardisation. The basic techniques of taking a flash picture are simple in themselves – the shutter has to open, the flash has to fire, the camera must be in a suitable position and a stop used to cover the distance within the tolerance of the film chosen. In ordinary photography, the possible permutations and margins for error are less above ground with the automated systems but they multiply underground because there are so many variables. Manufacturers of flash bulbs and electronic guns produce their own calculations for the known factors of their own forms of illumination. Flash bulb packets give the relevant information with what they call Guide Numbers in tables of apertures relevant to film speed and distance. To get the correct aperture or stop, there is a simple calculation – the guide number is divided by the distance in feet or metres. It follows that if the choice of stop is important for various reasons, by dividing the Guide Number by the stop the relevant distance the flash must be from the subject is established. And remember, it is the distance of the flash bulb from the subject that matters, not from the camera unless the flash happens to be camera-mounted. On electronic guns there is usually a rotating calculator disc which sets off ranges against stops for a given film speed and it is fairly easy to make a similar gadget with bold, clear figures to do the same for flash bulbs. The new computerised guns make this so much easier.

Up to this point, it all seems plain sailing but these factors have been devised by manufacturers for what they consider normal conditions of average-sized rooms to which criteria few, if any, caves and potholes, conform. In caving, there are so many imponderables. The requirements of a close-up in a small chamber or a

65 & 66 (left and above) Gypsum – calcium sulphate mineral – forming in certain dry sections of Mammoth Cave, USA. *National Park Service of the US Department of the Interior*

quick action picture of someone on a ladder are vastly different from those necessary to illuminate a long passage, a big shaft or a huge cavern area. Some cave scenery tends to absorb light. At other times glistening, white formations and water can increase the light factor by an intense degree. It is also worth remembering that under normal conditions the inverse square law relating to light operates in that it decreases with the distance from a light source with the square of that distance, i.e. a subject three feet away would only get one ninth of the light of a subject one foot away, or 1/16. Hence the need for opening up apertures or putting in extra flash to compensate for the immense fall-off.

With all this paraphernalia and the need for extending the range of flash, it is obvious that cave photography is best done with a unit operating on its own. Many cavers are reluctant to linger, often in uncomfortable situations, whilst the cameras and other gadgets are set up. To illustrate big areas requires dedicated team work often with people strung out ahead of the camera firing flashes from staggered positions to give the full impression of length or depth. The Guide Numbers from their flash point onwards to another part of the subject is still valid as it is still not the distance from the camera which counts. Errors of exposure will only be overcome with practice and, if the finances will run to it in terms of films and bulbs apertures can be bracketed up or down. If sophisticated multi- or remote flash is not available and the human method is undertaken, some training is necessary to get the

sequence right for opening the shutter and firing the flashes in that order and not the other way round. Small parties can also get away with leaving the shutter open with the camera on its tripod, going on to selected locations for flashing – being always careful to keep headlights directed away from the camera. Some of the hit-or-miss business may also be removed in cases where it is possible to use the 'hand-bashers' or nic-ad batteries used for cine photography. While they are quite heavy, they have many uses, the best being that it is possible to take a meter reading which helps to eliminate some of the variables. But it takes time and experience to get things right. For this reason it is a good thing to keep a log book or shot list of everything taken underground – place, time, film, exposure, conditions etc. for checking with the ultimate results. Over-exposed foreground, shadowy distant shapes, streaks of light – or even blank frames tell their own story and a well-kept log will help to eliminate these frustrating experiences.

Close-up photography using extension tubes is the field of the specialist studying the minutae of cave life. Here problems of exposure and parallax arise and, again, the makers' Guide Numbers do not necessarily apply. Oddly enough, it is necessary to increase the aperture or the light source proportionately to the degree of the extension tube. It may mean a difference of between a half or over two stops more, another factor being whether the light source is electronic flash or flash bulb. In some specialist work, a ring flash attachment is the answer to some of these problems

67 (left) Placing a person in the photograph gives a sense of dimension. Main Chamber, Stoke Lane Slocker, the Mendip Hills. *Sheena Stoddard*

68 (above) Ingenious adaptation of caving helmet to take cine-camera.

although this can produce other problems arising from the frontal mounting.

In many aspects of cave photography it is also useful to include something which will give some idea of the scale – cavers *in situ* will help to indicate the size of a cave or formation. Traditionally, a flash bulb or carton, match box or cigarette packet have often been used in this context although I tend to resent the latter. I don't like cave air polluted with stale tobacco smoke. Perhaps the best thing to use is a white, clearly marked plastic ruler which adds no great weight to the cave photographer's kit.

Finally, I must mention cine photography. Here, as in still photography, great strides have been made in improving equipment suitable for caving movies. In some respects, cine work is not quite as chancey as still photography since the cine cameraman usually works with portable lighting units which have powerful and constant outputs. These provide the opportunity of metering the light either automatically through the camera or moving around the scene with a hand-held meter which, as I have said, is also useful to the still photographer. As with still photography, protection of the equipment is vital, probably more so in the case of cine cameras. Hand-held camera work is sometimes less difficult with cine but a tripod should be with the equipment. Some cavers have also achieved remarkable results by ingeniously mounting the camera on a helmet bracket – but a side counterweight is necessary if the camera is attached over the ear. Choice of camera

is also a matter of expense, depending in addition on whether it is a club or individual purchase. For films intended for eventual professional showing such as TV, 16 mm stock is the best although excellent results have been obtained on 8 mm. One of my pictures shows Syd Perou with his trusty Bolex, an extremely strong camera producing films of a high professional quality. Second-hand ones may be picked up even now but need protection from moisture and grit. Other cameras specially made for underwater photography are also on the market and recently Eumig have produced their Nautica which is moderately priced, completely waterproof and also resistant to grit and particles of sand. A special sealing ring enables it to be used under water and another useful quality is its slight buoyancy. If 'live' sound is required with the films, this can add greatly to the weight of equipment carried. At this level, cave photography requires a specialist unit of dedicated cavers prepared to act as porters and take part in the action when required. Wherever possible, cine photography should be planned out well ahead. Time taken in preparing a shooting script is well spent and a shot list should be kept of the action. 'Wild film' and '*camera veritie*' are effective at times but a precise plan often produces the best results.

At the end of the day whether it be still or cine photography, never put off cleaning your equipment. It should be thoroughly aired, wiped, brushed or dusted and films should be processed as quickly as possible before any latent dampness causes deterioration or tackiness of the emulsion.

10
WHERE TO CAVE IN BRITAIN

I have mentioned elsewhere that potholing or caving is the only true form of exploration left in Britain. Nearly every weekend new discoveries are made, unsuspected

69 The amazing formations of Ogof Ffynnon Ddu, south Wales.

passages are found and old caves produce fresh and exciting possibilities of further development. Every issue of the caver's excellent news magazine, *Descent*, contains references to the unending search for something new as do the many other caving publications from various clubs and learned bodies associated with caving. With that in mind, it would be almost impossible to give a comprehensive list of all the caves and their extensions in each individual area. Most of the old caving guide books have little relevance to the present day. Because of the increasing numbers of people making trips underground, there is understandable concern that over-use, inconsiderate exploitation and downright vandalism, is harmful. It is true that things have become so bad in some areas especially with the litter problem that it has been suggested that clubs should 'adopt' certain caves and clean them out.

'Recorditis' is a bugbear that many sports have to endure and caving is no exception, it is part of the human condition which has led to the success of such volumes as the *Guinness Book of Records*. Prior to 1978 the longest cave system in Britain – measured by totting up the length of all the explored passages – was that splendid Welsh system Ogof Ffynnon Ddu in which I have spent many happy hours. But at the end of that year members of the Northern Pennine Club found the missing link joining the big Easegill Caverns, Lancaster Hole and Pippikin Pot on Casterton Fell. Now known as Link Pot, the discovery added another mile and a half to the interrelating systems, making their total length about 27 miles (43 kilometres) which is three miles longer than the Welsh system. I have no doubt that it won't be long before the Welsh cavers will push ahead to try and re-establish their premier title.

The main caving areas in the British Isles are in Derbyshire, Devon, the Furness coast, the Mendip Hills, Yorkshire, south Wales, Northern Ireland, Eire and Scotland.

Derbyshire

The Peak District is right on the doorstep of hundreds of potholers who live in the cities and towns on its fringe. Every variety and classification of cave and pothole can be found within a few miles' radius of the hub of this National Park at Castleton. In addition

70 One of the most impressive entrances of any British cave, with its portal more than 30 yards (27 metres) across and 50 feet (15 metres) high, is the northernmost cave on mainland Britain – Smoo or MacAllister's Cave near Durness in Sutherland. *Tony Oldham*

there are hundreds of mine shafts and passages which attract cavers in their role as industrial archaeologists. The lead mines of Derbyshire are among the oldest in the country, one of our oldest mines being Od'in Mine at the foot of Mam Tor (Shivering Mountain). One of the best known natural caverns in Derbyshire is Peak Cavern, now a show cave, once known as The Devil's Arse i' th' Peak, famed in song, verse and legend. Genuine cavers are allowed beyond the tourist limits and it is here that much of the pioneering work by cave divers was undertaken. There are show caves all round Castleton which give a hint to the general public of what cavers are seeking in their explorations, such as Speedwell Mine which is traversed in boats to the fancifully but erroneously named Bottomless Pit; Treak Cliff Cavern, the first cave in Europe to be lit by electricity; and the Blue John Mine, famed for the rare fluospar (Blue John stone). A little further away at Bradwell is Bagshawe Cavern, once a show cave and now used to initiate novices in comparative safety. There are many 'sporting' caves and pots – Eldon Hole, mentioned elsewhere, Nettle Pot, Giant's Hole,

P8, Carslwark, Oxlow which has its links with Mask-hill Mine and Giant's. In this area much work is still taking place through various sumps and new connections have been made in such places as my old favourite Nettle Pot. Sadly, Giant's has suffered at the hands of the developer in an effort to make it into a show cave to rival those down in Castleton. To do so, the landowner has blasted the well-known and masochistically loved entrance obstacles – The Curtain, Pillar Crawl and Backwash Sump pool making an easy walk-way of what once used to be a struggle. I always regarded these sections as a natural template which warned me that my girth was getting too big. One has also now to pay to get into this system. Derbyshire also has a number of caves of archaeological interest such as Windy Knoll at the top of the Winnats Pass; Elderbush in the Manifold Valley; Thirsthouse Cavern in Deep-dale, Kingsterndale, which has yielded a rich treasure trove of Romano-British articles; and a good example of a cave dweller's abode in Thor's Cave in the Mani-fold Valley. And, in 1980, diving has again been extremely active in various parts of the Peak.

Devon

Although Devon does not have a great deal of lime-stone, it is the home of some dedicated cavers. The main systems are Buckfastleigh and Pridhamsleigh. The area is perhaps best known for its association with the eminent geologist William Pengelly, FRS. It was in his memory that the Pengelly Cave Research Centre was established at Buckfastleigh in 1962 which has contributed greatly to the knowledge of caves, not only in Devon but elsewhere, and has also done good work in the realm of cave conservation. As with other areas, it also has its show caves – the most famous being Kent's Cavern at Torquay with its fine collection of prehistoric remains. The Devon caves such as the Reed-Baker system at Buckfastleigh are the homes of several varieties of native bats. The nearby Joint-Mitnor cave has produced this country's richest collection of interglacial bone deposits.

Furness Coast and Pennines

The Furness area of Lancashire contains a considerable amount of limestone, all near the coast. As with Devon there is hardly any ladder work or flood risks but it is an interesting area geologically. Whilst still west of the Pennines, there are other parts of Cumbria and Lancashire with copper and lead mines. Around Nenthead near Alston is a rich field for mining research. There are still the sporting possibilities of getting into one of Britain's most extraordinary mining achievements, the Nent Force Level, now sealed off. This has a number of shafts dropping into the 4½ mile (7 kilometre) Level between Nenthead and Alston. Much research has been done in this area by Peter Jackson and his father, who have produced a fascinating study of the complex workings of Smallclough mine.

The Mendip Hills

The Mendips claim to possess 'the oldest stately home' in Britain – Wookey Hole, home of our early forebears. It was on show to the public long before our landed gentry started opening their homes to pay the rent, rates and death duties. As far as exploration is concerned, it is the preserve of cave divers, the only people who can follow the river Axe along the thousands of feet of flooded passages. Triumph and tragedy have often gone hand in hand in this remarkable cave which is far beyond the tourist limits. As in the Peak District and Yorkshire, many of the caves of Mendip were known to miners long before archaeological work began. Lamb Lair (or Leer) was first mined in the seventeenth century. Swildon's is another of the great Mendip systems and there are other 'classics' such as GB cave and Stoke Lane Slocker and St Cuthbert's swallet at Priddy. Most of the best systems in this area are under strict control by various clubs but there is ample scope even so, away from the major systems.

75 (overleaf, left) **Streaming near sump 2 in Swildon's Hole, the Mendip Hills.** *Sheena Stoddard*

76 (overleaf, right) **Formations in Stoke Lane Slocker, the Mendip Hills.** *Sheena Stoddard*

Yorkshire

This huge area has been described as the 'cradle of British speleology'. As I have already mentioned, E.-A. Martel gave renewed impetus to the work of early pioneers. Even before Martel's visit, W. Boyd Dawkins and others had been probing this limestone country. John Birbeck and William Metcalfe made the first descent of what was then known as Helln Pot, now better known as Alum Pot, in 1847. They organised what could be described as Britain's first caving team, consisting of ten people, who made the descent of what they called 'this aweful Chasm' with ropes, planks, a windlass and a fire-escape belt. Also about that time Mr M.T. Farrer of Clapham, who owned the Ingleborough estates, was responsible for the earliest discoveries in what is now the Ingleborough Show Cave. Originally, it went in for only 70 feet (21 metres) but Farrer had a stalagmite dam removed to reveal more than a mile of passages and many magnificent formations. Farrer, a man of great courage, explored one of the earlier pools in 1837 by swimming with a candle in his cap and a rope around his body, probably the earliest reference to swimming in cave exploration. Other show caves at Stump Cross, Skirwith, Weathercote, White Scar and Yordas are well known to tourists. But the area is renowned for some of the hardest caving anywhere in the world with literally hundreds of caves and potholes. Disaster has brought notoriety to some of them such as Mossdale, Providence and Dow, Alum and Goyden. And I have already made reference to the lead Yorkshire gained in establishing the longest cave system in Britain with the Lancaster Hole, Pippikin Pot and Easegill. This is a reminder that Yorkshire has by no means yielded its last secrets and the county has some of the most vigorous campaigning cavers in the country.

Wales

Although organised caving was a bit of a late starter in the Principality, Welsh cavers and their neighbours have pushed explorations both in the north and south. Archaeologists and geologists were the first to venture into the Welsh underworld which is rich in legend and tradition. Some of the earliest prints of stalactites and stalagmites are of scenes in the cave on Caldy Island, formerly Ynys Pyr, opposite Tenby in Pembrokeshire. I should really say Dyfed following local government reorganisation but I prefer the old county names and they are still readily identifiable. The earliest cave explored in south Wales appears to be at Crawley Rocks, at Oxwich Bay near Swansea, where the remains of elephant, rhinoceros, ox and hyena were found. The first in the field of Welsh cave exploration were the Morgan brothers who discovered Dan-yr-

Ogof at the head of the Swansea Valley in 1912. It became a show cave but that did not stop further exploration and it was an attractive girl member of South Wales Caving Club who managed to get through a tight and tortuous crawl into a magnificent new series. The great names of south Wales of course are Ogof Ffynnon Ddu, Agen Allwedd, Pant Mawr – but there are many systems, old and new, being developed. There has been a tendency to overlook north Wales but the caving scene is extremely active in that area both by the NWCC and visiting clubs, particularly in the river Alyn area. But perhaps one of the most exciting finds of recent years and which was a closely guarded secret whilst early exploration was made, was the finding, in 1971 of Otter Hole in the Wye Valley. This is probably the only limestone cave in the world which required consultation of a tide table

prior to a trip as the Wye is a tidal river and expeditions had to adjust their time tables because of the flooding of the sump. The Royal Forest of Dean Caving Club has done an excellent job in this system. Not the least of the mysteries they unravelled was the eerie sounds produced by the receding waters.

Ireland

One of the finest caving areas I have been in has been Ireland, both north and south. Whilst a good deal of the explorations over there have been by teams from this side of the Irish Sea, there is a growing and enthusiastic caving fraternity based in Belfast and in Dublin. The upland areas of limestone in Ireland have a haunting, remote beauty of their own and the underworld is dramatic and colourful. I was introduced to it by the late Mr J.C. Coleman of the Irish Tourist Board who did so much to popularise the sport over there. I treasure his personal gift of *The Caves of*

Ireland, the first really comprehensive collation of nearly 300 caves. As with other caving areas, the first explorations were made by archaeologists and geologists and it is only in comparatively recent times that cavers have been active across the water. Even here can be found the names of the inexhaustible Frenchman, Edouard-Alfred Martel, and our own Ernest Baker. Martel's book, *Ireland et les Cavernes Anglaises*, first published in 1897, included some of the better known systems and also dramatic sketches of such great caves as Marble Arch in Fermanagh which, I heard recently, may be made into a show cave.

The Irish underworld contains mile after mile of passages and formations to match and, at times, surpass those in other parts of the world. One of the earliest references to a cave is at Dunmore in Kilkenny, mentioned in AD 928 in *The Annals of the Four Masters*. Its ancient name was Derc Ferna meaning the Cave of the Alders and was reputedly the scene of the slaughter of a thousand people. The terminology of Irish caves has the same fascination of those of Wales and Scotland and the prefix *poll* implies a hole in the ground or cave. It is a little confusing to find there are at least ten Pollnagollums (Cave of the Doves); the Pollnagollum-Polleva system is probably the best known on the bare limestone of the Slieve Elva in County Clare. The main caving areas in the south are in Kilkenny, Laoighis, Tipperary, Kerry, Cork, Waterford and Mayo; Sligo, Leitrim, Fermanagh and Cavan in the north. It is worth bearing in mind that a number of Irish cave systems are subject to flash flooding and I once had a long wait to get out of Pollnagollum. Also, for serious archaeological excavations it is necessary to get permission from the Commissioners of Public Works as caves come under the general protection of the National Monuments Act. The longest cave, with a tremendous potential is Reyfad Pot in County Fermanagh. First discovered by the Yorkshire Ramblers' Club in 1939, the past few years have seen tremendous development.

Scotland

Scotland has been something of a Cinderella of British caving, neglected until recent years. Many of the country's best known caves are not in limestone at all, such as Fingal's Cave in the basalt of Staffa and Bruce's Cave at Kirkpatrick Fleming, Dumfriesshire, where Robert Bruce is reputed to have watched that indefatigable spider which inspired him to further battle against the English. In recent years work by the Grampian Speleological Group and Glasgow Speleological Society has boosted the known and explored caves in Scotland to around 500, many of them in the remote and lovely hills of Sutherland and the other western mountain areas. In my book *Caving* published in 1969, I predicted that discoveries in the valleys of the Tralligill and Allt Nan Uamh could do bigger and better things and this has been proved correct. Scotland now provides some excellent caving – its deepest at the time of writing being the Cnoc nan Uamh in the Assynt area and Uamh nan Claig-ionn, the then deepest pothole. Cavers in Scotland face some extremely hard work to get to their locations, often around 2000 feet (610 metres) up steep mountain sides. There are also many caves on the islands, mostly formed by the sea and erosion, such as Skye which has quite a number.

There are five main limestone caving areas in Scotland.

81 **Famed in words, music and art, Fingal's Cave on Staffa which has inspired such men as Mendelssohn, Turner, Sir Walter Scott, Wordsworth, Robert Louis Stevenson and Jules Verne.** *Tony Oldham*

82 The Isle of Skye has many caves. Spar cave on the coast at Glasnakille, south-east of Elgol, has developed some remarkable formations. Its traditional name Slochd Altrimen has been known for a thousand years. *Tony Oldham*

The furthest north is at Durness and Assynt in Sutherland, a wonderful and wild mountain area. Here are Cambrian limestone systems with classic karst basins. Applecross and Loch Kishorn areas have small caves in the Jurasssic oolitic and Cambrian limestones with one over 1000 feet (305 metres) long at Applecross. The area around Glencoe has always been famous for its mountaineering and it is only in recent years that many exciting discoveries have been made in the hills of Appin, south of Ballachhulish. These metamorphic limestones contain some of Scotland's most sporting caves and potholes as well as being geomorphologically interesting. Skye, the fourth caving area, also contains Cambrian and Jurassic limestones with literally hundreds of small caves and two at least of a length greater than 1000 feet (305 metres). These are mainly near Broadford in the south of the island. The fifth area is around the delightful sugar loaf mountain Schiehallion which towers above Loch Rannoch. Around its base are the Blair Atholl metamorphic limestones with vadose stream passages of considerable interest. Cave divers have been active in many areas but mostly in the north in the Sutherland caves and important discoveries have been made by Tony Boycott and Martyn Farr notably in the Cnoc nan Uamh caves. To anyone caving in Scotland far from the wellworn caving tracks further south I would echo the greeting of the Grampian Speleological Group: 'Latha math qheibh fo'n talamh' – (Have a nice day underground).

General

From the foregoing it will be apparent that there are literally thousands of caves and potholes throughout the British Isles and many more awaiting to be discovered. There are others which are completely artificial – my home town of Stockport has a vast rabbit warren of sandstone passages created to form air-raid shelters in the last war. Nor do all of them have respectable histories. Although they are classed as 'caves', the caverns at West Wycombe in Buckinghamshire are part of a chalk mine originally created to provide work for unemployed villagers. The caves became the venue for the Hell Fire Club which included famous politicians of the day masquerading as the Monks of Medenham. In 1763 John Wilkes was prosecuted for obscene libel after his famous *Essay on Women*. It revealed a big political scandal which shocked the British public when they learned that many of its leaders indulged in strange practices and mysterious rites with courtesans who called themselves nuns. Today, the cave has been decked out with figures from the past depicting scenes of debauchery and a visit by no less respectable a person than Benjamin Franklin in 1773 which may have inspired him to invent the lightning conductor to divert wrath from on high for such a sordid sojourn.

CAVES OF THE WORLD

Whilst this book is a partly historical and a partly practical guide to those who wish to take up the sport of caving in Britain, it would be totally inadequate without some reference to the great caving areas of the world, many of which have been visited and explored in recent years by British teams. Few countries of the world are without caves of one form or another. Cavers are mainly concerned with exploration in limestone and associated rock structure but there are caves in sandstone, lava and even ice. And of course, there are many caverns under the sea which, in a few million years and geological movement may be revealed in a new landmass. With reference to ice caves, recent years have seen the growth of glacio-speleology with interest being stimulated by Dr William Halliday who has made a special study of the Paradise Ice caves on Mount Rainier, the 14,408 foot (439 metre) dormant volcano in the Cascade Range in West Central Washington. At the time of writing this was the longest mapped ice cave in the world, around 8 miles (13 kilometres). As I was studying the background to these caves and other ice passages in America, I came across a remarkable coincidence, that the pioneer of glacio-speleology in America was called Balch – Edwin Swift Balch – the same surname as that great Mendip caver, Herbert Ernest Balch. Equally coincidental is that they were both investigating caves in two greatly different environments at about the same time at the turn of this century. Caves in ice are a well-known phenomenon – I have found several in Norway – and glacio-speleology is an intriguing specialist branch of caving with many areas to investigate from Europe to Antarctica.

Similarly, lava caves caused by the other extreme, heat and the molten outpourings of volcano, is another specialist subject on which tremendous work remains to be done. Lava caves of varying size in the active and inert volcanic regions of the world – the United States, Japan, Africa, Iceland, Europe and the Canary Isles are the most generally known. There is, in connection with lava caves, a delightful Hawaiian name – *pahoehoe* – the ropy or corded lava in which cave-type tubes are formed. Volcano-speleology has a growing band of devotees, and exploration in this direction could lead to a greater understanding of our nearer planets where space exploration has revealed that some of them have been subject to similar basaltic volcanism aeons ago. Lava caves have already produced a number of surprising finds, not the least in Rhinoceros Cave in the area of the Grand Coulee dam in Washington. There, paleontologists made the exciting discovery of the bones of the giant American rhinoceros buried in a lava exudation millions of years ago and long extinct on that continent.

United States of America

Traditionally, cave exploration has always been associated with Europe and, more particularly, France where the science of speleology had its foundation. It was only in fairly recent years and due to the growing international links between cavers that there became an awareness of the amount of caving activity in the so-called New World, America. It has even been claimed that the Founding Father of America, George Washington, may well have been the father of speleology, or spelunking as they call it, as well. In a cave which bears his name, are the revered letters 'G. Washington, 1748' and there is sufficient evidence to show that the first president, a capable surveyor, was at least near that cave above Evitt's Run in the Virginian bluegrass country in March of that year. When a Masonic lodge bought the cave for their secret rites only twenty-five years after that date, there are the names of two Washingtons on the conveying deed. Even if 'G. Washington, 1748' is a forgery, it is still pretty ancient, as it was referred to in print as far back as 1833. If there is doubt as to whether the first president was an active caver, there is none about the interest of the third president's interest in the subterranean world. Thomas Jefferson published a history of Virginia in 1784 which included the first map of any cave in North America – or the world for that matter – of Madison's Cave where George Washington also left his signature; this one more authentic. If he had not become president, Jefferson would still be remembered in the academic world of paleolontology for *Megalonyx jeffersoni*. Salpetre miners, who had ventured into caves long before Washington's date to find the basic ingredient of gunpowder, discovered the skeleton of a large animal in Organ Cave, West Virginia. The bones

83 The Crystal Grotto near Mo i Rana, Nordland, Norway. *Harry Strokkenes*

were shown to Jefferson who deduced that it had been a creature with a long claw such as an immense lion or other member of the Felidae (cat family). It was finally established as the genus *chloleopus*, a type of ground sloth with long claws extinct for thousands of years – and it is still classified under the name of Jefferson.

So caving in North America had its earliest beginnings in Virginia and it was in Kentucky that the world's biggest cave system was discovered about 1799; controversy still surrounds the date. One version asserts that Mammoth Cave was first entered by a pioneer named Hutchins or Houchins in pursuit of a wounded bear – a court record gives it as 1809 – although it was probably known to the Indians, as other cave were, long before then. It is, however, more likely that prospecting saltpetre miners made the historic discovery, potassium nitrate being vital as a basis for explosives, and a Land Registry item of 14 September 1798 mentions it as a saltpetre cave. It was the search for this valuable nitre for gunpowder to help sustain the War of Independence against the British that miners and geologists went further and further into this vast complex of caves. But systematic exploration probably only began with the cave's first guide, curiously enough, a negro slave called Stephen Bishop who died in July 1857 although his 'official' tombstone showed it to be two years later. Bishop was the first to go beyond one of the world's many 'bottomless' pits and, as the years went by, there was a growing belief that Mammoth had a connection with Flint Ridge. Mammoth, Flint and Elko Ridges form a triumvirate of great plateau ridges laid down 200 million years ago when most of what is now Kentucky and neighbouring States were being formed under the shallow Mississippian Sea.

It is to the credit of a great number of dedicated American cavers that years of laborious and often dangerous exploration finally came to successful fruition in 1972. On 30 August a Cave Research Foundation team led by a twenty-nine-year-old Massachussets housewife, Mrs Patricia P. Crowther discovered the connection between Flint Ridge cave system and Mammoth Cave. On 10 September another CRF team, this time led by John P. Wilcox, a mechanical engineer and CRF director, made the first port-to-portal trip. As this was an achievement comparable to climbing Everest, I feel the names of the other members of the teams should be given. The through team included P. Gary Eller, a banjo-playing PhD in chemistry; Cleveland F. Pinnix, a BA in English literature, Stephen G. Wells, a geology graduate and Richard P. Zopf, a carpenter and craftsman. The survey team consisted of Mrs Crowther, Wilcox, Zopf and Thomas A. Bruckner then a nineteen-year-old student and the CRF's youngest

84 Echo River outlet where the major underground stream surfaces. Mammoth Cave National Park. *National Park Services of the US Department of the Interior*

elected member. At the time of writing, the Flint-Mammoth linking up contains 190 miles (307 kilometres) of passages. Even now, further exploration has added to the ever growing length of this cave system which now has at least twenty entrances. The theory has been advanced that it could reach a length of 300 miles (483 kilometres). In this land of superlatives, it comes as no surprise to read the assertion of Professor N.S. Shaler, former State geologist for Kentucky that there are at least 100,000 miles (160,934 kilometres) of open caverns beneath the surface of the State's carboniferous limestone. More than a hundred years ago the American poet George Dennison Prentice captured the awe he felt in Mammoth Cave . . .

High pillar'd domes,
   With stars and flowers all fretted like halls
Of Oriental monarchs . . . rivers dark
   and drear and voiceless as oblivion's stream,
That flows through death's dime vale of
         silence . . . gulfs
   All fathomless, down which the loosened rock
Plunges until its far-off echoes come
   Fainter and fainter like the dying roll
Of thunder in the distance. . . . Stygian pools
   Whose agitated waves give back a sound
Hollow and toneless, like the sullen roar
   In the volcano's depths . . . these, these have left
Their spell upon me, and their memories
   Have passed into my spirit, and are now
Blent with my being until they seem a part
   of my own immortality.

Effusive, not exactly Walt Whitman but a powerful reaction to a powerful situation.

A recent survey has revealed that there could be up to 50,000 caves across the States so it is evident that the United States must have the greatest concentration of caves in the world. Like Mammoth Cave, many of them are now show caves although they also provide for the sporting and scientific cavers whose work adds to the growing store of knowledge. Eight of the world's twenty longest caves are in the United States although it does not have one in the deepest twenty – you have to go south of the border for the deep ones. Among the most famous are Carlsbad Caverns discovered by a wandering cowboy Jim White in New Mexico in 1901, notable for its immense formations and bats. Luray caves in Virginia are really for the tourists but I mention them because they contain a caving curio, probably the strangest musical instrument in the world, a 'stalacpipe organ' which produces music when electrically triggered rubber hammers strike stalactites which have been ground to pitch. It is not unusual for the strains of the Wedding March from *Lohengrin* to be heard in this labyrinth played at a number of subterranean marriage ceremonies. Ah well, I suppose it could only happen in the USA. Still

85 Typical dry passage at Mammoth Cave. *National Park Service of the US Department of the Interior*

on a musical note I once mentioned to Sir John Barbirolli that stalactites made pleasant tinkling sounds when struck gently and he was intrigued at the possibility of a concerto for formations and the Halle Orchestra. He ruled it out saying, 'I don't think we could get the 'bull' (bass) fiddle down there.' But orchestras do play in some of the world's show caves. Show caves with special features are Wind Cave in South Dakota which gets its name from the air which rushes into or out of the cavern as the barometric pressure rises or falls; and Cathedral Caverns in Alabama's Appalachian foothills which contains 'Goliath', claimed to be the world's mightiest stalagmite estimated to be 125 million years old.

For the real cave explorer nearly every State has exciting sporting and scientific possibilities – the water-filled grottoes of Florida which beckon the cave diver, lava caves in California and Oregon. Even the small caves such as Ogle Cave – small by American standards – in the Guadalupe Mountains of New Mexico are dreams come true for photographers. Hawaii, the youngest State way out in the North Pacific has its own special caving interest in its lava tubes. Kazamura cave has been mapped for over five miles and, in 1979 a British speleological expedition went out to the Kilauea and Mauna Loa volcanoes to make a special study of lava tube systems based, as I mentioned earlier, on the possible relation between volcanic events on Earth and those which space exploration has revealed on the planets. Mauna Kea is remarkable in many ways, being not only the highest island mountain in the world, 13,825 feet (4214 metres) but is also considered to be the highest individual mountain on Earth, above even Mount Everest, if its true height is reckoned from its base in the North Pacific, which is over 32,000 feet (9754 metres). New information from the various probes revealed that the Nix Olympica had the same structure as the Hawaiian volcanoes and that the Martian 'shield' volcano Olympus Mons towered to a height of 17 miles (27 kilometres).

Mexico to South America

British cavers must envy their American spelunking cousins. For, in addition to their own vast and varied cave systems, it is not too difficult for them to journey south, still on the North American landmass, to Mexico. Its 761,000 square miles (1,970,990 square kilometres) contains one of the largest limestone regions in the world, the limestone extending deep into South America itself. Mexican exploration was fairly limited until the 1960s, when Texan cavers crossed the border lured by information about deep pits. Cenotes – potholes partially filled with water – were known for hundreds of years. For some time, the best known of the Mexican 'deeps' was the Sotano de las Golindras,

86 Cleveland Avenue, an elliptical passageway with gypsum 'flowers' on ceiling and walls. *National Park Services of the US Department of the Interior*

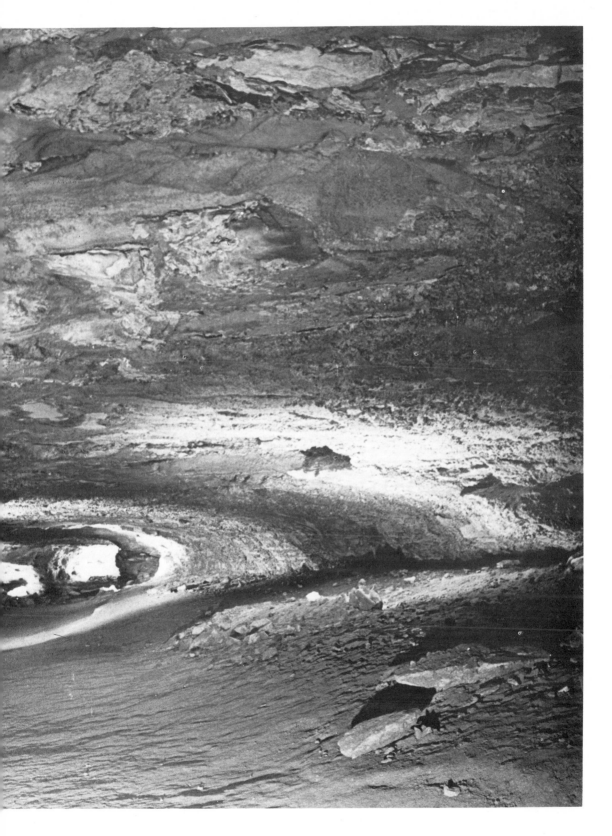

1680 feet (512 metres) in the central LSP region. It was here that SRT techniques came into their own and were used for descent and ascent. Now there are at least twelve caves over 1640 feet (500 metres) deep with prospects that at least one of them will pass the 3280 feet (1000 metre). This is the Sistema de la Purificacion in the Sierra de Tamaulipas north-west of Tampico. The longest and deepest cave in Mexico, it resulted from the link-up between the Cueva del Brinco and the Cueva del Infiernello and my latest information was that it had been pushed to nearly 2930 feet (893 metres). There are other deep shafts in the Tamaulipas area; Queretaro north-west of Mexico City; and further north in Chiuahua around Guerrero more caves have been discovered in Chilpancingo region with some of the best caving in the country at Cuetzalan, Puebla in the high limestone region near Popocatepetl. At Cuetzalan the Sistema de Chichicazapan-Atichayan is also heading for the 1000 metre class with possible linkage with adjoining caves. Further south, in Oaxaca at Huautla the Sotano de San Augustin reached a sump at 2818 feet (859 metres) and could yield more if dived beyond. And the country's third and fourth deepest caves, the Sotano de Agua de Carrizo and the adjacent La Grieta, if joined could go beyond 2953 feet (900 metres). Right at the tail end of the country Chiapas State and the Yucatan Peninsula have growing possibilities for exploration with the likelihood that the Actung Kaua complex could extend for up to 20 miles (32 kilometres).

Continuing south into Guatemala, the limestone continues to be thick and full of caving potential as is its neighbouring Chiapas. El Cimarron used to be the country's deepest shaft at 600 feet (183 metres) but deeper drops have been found in the area of Barillas in northern Huehuetegnango. The Cueva de Agua Escondida is described as a superb river cave with a strong current making exploration difficult.

Little seems to be known of caves through the Honduras, Nicaragua, Costa Rica and Panama but there are belts of limestone there which seem to have been by-passed by cave explorers. On the South American continent itself, even today much of the landmass remains unexplored, let alone the underground areas. Venezuela is almost virgin caving territory with most significant finds being made along the Cordo Merida range and deep caves in the high and remote Sarisarinama plateau. Some caves have been reported in the strange uplands of the Pakaraima Mountains between Venezuela and Guyana – the so-called Lost World.

For all its immense 3¼ million square miles (8,417,500 square kilometres), Brazil has not yet contributed a great deal to the pursuit of caving knowledge. Such limestone as is known is in the lower reaches of the Amazon. In the higher lands Professor Marcel Homet found tombs and painted caves but no really deep shafts. According to that indefatigable chronicler of

caves the deepest in Brazil was the Gouffre de Tobias in Sao Paolo at 470 feet (143 metres) although it is thought to be deeper. Such deep cavities as are known are along the river Ouro Grosso and the Agua Suja and the Sao Mateus cave has been recorded as 8 miles (13 kilometres) long.

Further east Peru has had no prolonged siege of its undoubtedly deep limestone – the 4000 mile (6437 kilometre) length of the Andes has thick bands of limestone and there is little doubt that there are potholes of immense depth as they start at considerable height. Only the area beyond Lima seems to have been prospected so far at around 13,000 feet (3900 metres) and the only named cave of any depth is the Sima de Milpo discovered and explored by a British team in 1972 to a depth of 1335 feet (407 metres).

Tiny Ecuador made little impact on the caving world until 1976 when a British army expedition which took along cavers more or less as an afterthought, plus no less, Neil Armstrong who had been the first man on the moon. The inspiration behind all this was the book *The Gold of the Gods* by Erich von Däniken. Like Conan Doyle, he had an imaginative feeling about the subterranean world and visualised thousands of miles of tunnels under Ecuador. Science fiction stuff, it presupposed these were created by visiting spacemen, hence Neil Armstrong, with their equivalent of thermal lances and lasers. Immense wealth lay buried deep in the limestone at the Cueva de Los Tayos in the Morona-Santiago region somewhere in the heart of an equatorial rain forest. The British cavers did, in fact, find the cave described by Däniken but little else except that the Jivaro Indians of the area had made previous descents on vine creepers with bamboo torches in pursuit of baby oil birds or tayos. Serious work was done, however, to shade in a little more of the map of the underground regions of the world and others may be tempted to this remote corner for further study and adventures.

Further south still through the long straggle of Chile, Patagonia down to Tierra del Fuego is more or less *terra incognita* for cavers, although the geological surveys I have indicate limestone in some form or another right down to the tip of the continent. A climber friend of mine also told me of some small caves around Mount Adam in the Falkland Islands but he was too disinterested to take much notice of them!

Cavers who often endure cold and wet climates in pursuit of their pastime will find the Greater Antilles in the Caribbean a delightful change. The limestone stretching out through Mexico's Yucatan Peninsula seems to continue through this island chain to Cuba, Haiti and Puerto Rico. In fact, the Cuban President Fidel Castro was once an active caver and has since encouraged speleological studies on the island. Both the caves of Juara and Jibara are over 876 feet (217 metres) deep and Santo Tomas cavern is in the league of the world's longest with around 20 miles (32 kilometres) of passages; there are many more which would yield to persistent exploration. Jamaica is also fortunate in having its own active caving organisations and, for its size, the island has an intense concentration of caves and sinkholes, several hundred in fact. Many of these in that geologically freakish area of the Cockpit Country. Underground rivers abound, many with numerous cascades, the most spectacular of which is the Quashies river cave.

Canada

Canada was something of a late starter in the realm of speleological exploration in anything like an organised way. Old caves and shelters were known about in various parts of the country and tentatively explored. Occasionally, geologists showed an interest in the limestone areas but it took a few expatriate British speleologists to get things going, notably that learned former Mendip caver Derek Ford who became Professor of Geography at McMaster University, Hamilton, in 1964. He played an inspirational part in the exploration of Canada's potholes and caves along with such other notable cavers from England as Mike Boon

and Peter Thompson; the latter becoming editor of the excellent *Caving International Magazine*. From the mid-1960s caving has proceeded apace. The caves of Canada reach almost from sea-board to sea-board, not in a continuous link, I hasten to add. They are grouped in the Atlantic region from Anticosta Island, Quebec and Ontario in the east to the Rockies, The North West Territories and British Columbia in the west. The first recorded descent of any note seems to have been made by the Canadian mountaineer and surveyor A.O. Wheeler and other members of the Canadian Alpine Club in their explorations of the Columbian icefield. As far back as 1912 they found and descended Arctomys Cave near Jasper in what is now the Mount Robson provincial park. Not being cavers nor equipped for cave exploration, they retreated at the first serious obstacle, a waterfall at 250 feet (76 metres) down. Some years earlier, Wheeler had shown an interest in the Nakimu Caves in what is now the Glacial National Park of British Columbia and whose fate it was to become exploited as an early show cave

87 The Straw Gallery, Arctomys Cave, Canada.
P. Thompson

being handily placed for the Canadian Pacific Railway. By any standards, Arctomys is a remarkable cave whose full potential became apparent to the McMaster University Karst Research Group. Following its full exploration in 1971, Actomys Cave established a new North American depth record on 1715 feet (523 metres). Whilst it is not regarded as an excessively difficult cave – the longest of its five pitches is only 50 feet (15 metres) – it is difficult to reach unless a helicopter is used. It is also one of Canada's longest systems, at 17,277 feet (5266 metres).

In Alberta in the Banff National Park, Castleguard Cave, apart from being the best known of the Canadian caves, is also something of an oddity in that its 'descent' eventually means a gradual climb inside the noble Mount Castleguard in the area bounded by the Saskatchewan and south glaciers. Castleguard Cave has a variety of caving problems, including the risk of flooding, and its entrance above the Castleguard valley was visited in the 1920s. Again, the first obstacle, a 28 foot (8 metre) drop probably put off the early visitors. It leads into a 'duck' or an icy slide, depending on the time of year. A normal caving trip in Castleguard takes about two days to do the whole length and stops when one is literally banging one's head on the underside of the Columbia Icefield which covers over 100 square miles (259 square kilometres). Despite its remoteness and the difficulties of the cave itself, Castleguard still excites interest and it may yet yield more secrets – it is Canada's longest cave at 43,000 feet (13,106 metres). The latest I heard was that the surveyed length had been extended to 46,000 feet (14 kilometres) and draughts in various sections are clues to further developments. Because of its location, its true depth is not likely to exceed 1018 feet (310 metres) between the entrance and the ice-blockage, although there could be other passages higher up in Mount Castleguard. Some day in the distant future it is possible that a caver could emerge on to the icefield itself but it will take a lot of glacial recession before that happens. Unfortunately, Castleguard came in for some of that bureaucratic interference which is irksome not only to cavers but other free-ranging souls. The park authorities, quite arbitrarily, decided that caving was too dangerous and that the inexperienced, stimulated by an excellent film about the cave, might rush in and create rescue problems. Admission was restricted to a permit system. This, in the land of pioneers!

My Canadian friends may feel I have dealt excessively with just two great caves at the expense of many other fine ones. Some of them echo nostalgia for Britain's own caves where some of the new Canadian cavers cut

88 (left) The Pendulum, Straw Gallery, Arctomys Cave. *P. Thompson*

89 (above) Ice heaves in Castleguard Cave. *Derek Ford*

their teeth – Yorkshire Pot, Derbyshire Pot and Mendip Cave in the Crowsnest Pass area at the southern end of the Rockies. On the western side of the country still, Vancouver Island has a fair number of caves dotted all over; The North West Territories (in which I have a special interest due to the explorations of a former fellow townsman of mine, Admiral Sir George Back), has little caving interest except near the border with the Yukon. From the east moving inland, caves have been explored in Newfoundland, Nova Scotia, Quebec and Ontario. the latter State claimed the longest cave in the eastern part of the country – Moira Cave which extends for over 6500 feet (1980 metres).

Australia and New Zealand

The vast continent of Australia and its neighbour, New Zealand, like Canada, has seen a rapid growth in cave exploration in the past few years where some fine indigenous cavers have emerged. But limestone and its associated caverns was found very early in the settlement of Australia. The rock was searched for primarily to create the mortar for the building of the penal colony at Sydney Cove. Records reveal that an expedition set forth to find this vital commodity in October 1804. At the end of that year the expedition leader, Colonel William Paterson was able to report to Governor Philip King the finding of a considerable area of limestone at the mouth of the Tamar River in what was Van Diemans Land, now better known as Tasmania. Whilst no record appears to have been made at the time, the island across the Bass Strait has become one of the main caving areas in the Southern Hemisphere. On the mainland itself, another expedition trying to find a route from Australia's own Liverpool to Jervis Bay wandered into Bungonia Creek and found another limestone area, now well known for its caves and is now a Cave Reserve. From the early 1800s onwards, history had a fairly well-documented history of caverns in then remote, but now more populous, parts of the south-east. In fact some of the earliest artistic paintings of caves come from the Australian continent, coincidentally enough by two succeedings artists with Charles Darwin on HMS *Beagle* – Augustus Earle and Conrad Martens. Archaeological research has shown that Australia was colonised and had cave communities during the antipodean Ice Age with the finding and carbon dating of charcoal associated with stone tools at Kenniff Cave in the Queensland Great Dividing Range.

The greatest concentration of known caves is in the south-eastern corner in New South Wales with the great show caves of Jenolan, Yarrangobilly and Bungonia and the Wombeyan caves of the central tableland of New South Wales. Further south in Victoria there are good caving possibilities with the greatest prehistorical interest in Cloggs Cave at Buchan with its evidence of such extinct fauna as the giant kangaroo, the Tasmanian wolf and that nocturnal carnivorous marsupial, the Tasmanian devil. But the most fascinating area is the Nullabor Plain which lies about two-thirds in southern Australia and a third in western Australia. It is probably the world's greatest karst area spreading over some 77,200 square miles (199,948 square kilometres) lying between the Great Victoria Desert to the north and the waters of the Great Australian Bight in the south. This is no weekend caving country – it is about equidistant from the two biggest centres of population, Perth and Adelaide, each nearly 1000 miles (1609 kilometres) away. During the past few years the growing band of Australian cavers have attacked this area with great success and, despite the remoteness of the area, have found time to explore over 200 caves, some of immense proportions. The biggest and best known is Mullamullang Cave with its exceptionally large passages and chambers, underground sand dunes, rare gypsum and halite or rock salt, evidence of the evaporation of subterranean saline waters which still remain in this area forming beautiful blue lakes. Whilst the caves are difficult to reach, they have a rare attraction for cavers for other reasons than pure exploration – the underground temperature is almost constant at 19°C (66.2°F) and a humidity of 75 per cent. It is in this region that extremely long dives are possible as some of the caves have literally miles of water-filled passages. Cave diving, which began in Australia in 1952 has developed tremendously since then and the claim has been made that Australia really holds the cave diving record of 6562 feet (2000 metres) in Cocklebiddy Cave – and the water passage just goes on and on. The last I heard in 1979 was that this cave had been dived to nearly 2½ miles (almost four kilometres) but the inhibiting factors for further exploration is the sheer length and the expense of the equipment and manpower needed to reach the limits of this water passage.

In the south-west tip of the continent, there are a few small, beautifully decorated caves such as Easter Cave near Augusta with pendulite formations of stalactite. This cave has now been explored for over 6 kilometres and still has possibilities. Above the 25° latitude, caves are sparsely scattered. Some are interesting mainly for their links with primitive man or their ecosystems such as Mount Etna near Rockhampton with its bat population of about half a million. In addition to its limestone caves, Australia has also had a volcanic past and both Victoria and Queensland have lava tunnels. Apart from Nullarbor, the main sporting interest of Australian cavers is off the mainland in Tasmania which contains the longest and deepest caves first tackled by the Tasmanian Caverneering Club which was founded as far back as 1946. The entrances are as hard to find as those in Norway, hidden as they are in well-wooded mountains. In this context, an acquaintance with Professor J.R.R. Tolkien's works would be helpful. Khazad-dûm, the Dwarf-hall home of Durin's Folk, gives its name to Tasmania's deepest shaft which has been pushed to 1053 feet (321 metres). Mole Creek Cave contains the largest stalagmite, Kubla Khan and the longest system is Exit Cave, at 55,774 feet (17 kilometres).

Both North and South islands of New Zealand have some fine caves and a growing caving community. On North Island the main caving area is at Waitomo where there are a number of impressive stream caves notable for a special breed of glow-worm unique to this part of the Southern Hemisphere. They exist in such large clusters that they give enough light for cavers to see by. The longest is Gardiner's Gut at over 8½ miles (about 14 kilometres). The best caving, however, is in the cold, vertical systems in the smooth, pressured limestone better known as marble on South Island. The marble is concentrated in the Tasman Mountains around Mount Arthur, Mount Owen and Takaka Hill. New Zealand and Australian cavers have produced many finds and the area has great potential. Harwood Hole on Takaka Hill, which has a 577 foot (176 metre) entrance pitch, has been explored to 1171 feet (357 metres) and Greenlink Cave down to 1207 feet (368 metres). As the marble covers over 30 square miles (80 square kilometres) and is up to nearly 6550 feet (200 metres) thick the possibilities seem to be endless especially in a new cave called Nettlebed with a depth of 948 feet (289 metres) and a length of over 3¼ miles (6 kilometres).

South-East Asia

North of Australia and heading for South-East Asia there is another exciting new caving area where recent expeditions have found vast new fields to conquer. Borneo, New Guinea and Sumatra have been the recent targets for caving adventure and discovery in great areas of virgin limestone. These inaccessible regions are now opening up with the encouragement of the governments concerned. New Guinea has seen a steady procession of cavers over the past sixteen years from Australia, Europe and Japan and much more is now known. The island is almost equally divided into jungle and swampy land and a mountain chain that runs for some 1100 miles (1770 kilometres) reaching a height of 16,404 feet (5000 metres). Papua New Guinea has been emerging from its shrouded past and the expeditions I have mentioned have only scratched the surface. Prospecting for new caves has always been difficult due to the dense vegetation but aerial surveys have shown sinkholes and disappearing rivers. A two-man team, New Zealander Van Watson, and a New Guinea man, Kevan Wilde, made the first significant big drop of 1621 feet (494 metres) in Bibima Cave. Further exploration in the Muller Range of mountains led to Atea Kananda which, in 1978 had been surveyed to a distance of 19 miles (30¼ kilometres) and 6 miles (10 kilometres) longer than Selminum Tem in the nearly 2000 foot (600 metres) high Hindenburg Wall. Deep drops have since been discovered in the Napeanai Mountains and further big discoveries are expected from another major expedition in 1982.

It was known by the middle of the last century that Borneo had a considerable number of caves and they were first described by that intrepid explorer Spenser St John. Little was heard of them for over a hundred years until G.E. Wilford of the Malaysian Geographic Survey made a special study of the limestone under the rain forests and made the first exploratory descents. Sufficient was published to excite outside interests and encourage expeditions in the 1970s. The most successful was in 1977–8 sponsored by the Royal Geographical Society to the area around Mount Mulu in northern Sarawak on the edge of the Penambo Range. This is in the Gunung Mulu National Park which was created more with the intention of conservation than tourist exploitation. There are many caves in the humid, dripping uplands whose rainfall of 400 inches (1016 cm) a year is one of the shaping factors in the growth of underground passages. There are now more than 30 miles (48 kilometres) of surveyed caves in this area including the Gua Terangair – Clearwater Cave, believed to be the longest known outside Europe and North America with 16 miles (26 kilometres) of passages; and it could be even longer. Gua Payau (Deer Cave) contains what is regarded as the world's largest cave passage in terms of all-round size with a width of 571 feet (174 metres) and a height of 400 feet (122 metres). With such a rainfall, it is inevitable that many of the caves are subject to flooding but there is no need to wear clothing to keep out the cold – the water has been known to reach 80°F (27°C). Cave life abounds, including one of the eighteen species of Salangane (*Collocalia*) or swiftlet which gets its name from the tiny island of Salangan in the Malaya archipelago. But this is not the variety which exists in the Niah Great Cave about 80 miles (128 kilometres) to the south-west which provides the basic ingredient for bird's nest soup. It is this substance, made of gummy bird spittle, which accounts for the primitive people of Borneo having knowledge of their caves – at least the entrances – as they sought this delicacy, venturing underground with torches and ladders made from bamboo and rattan rope. These birds are likewise found in Java and Timor which should also produce a rewarding cave study. I am told that the Padang Highlands of western Sumatra has enough limestone to be worthy of investigation too.

It is not beyond the bounds of possibility that there should be caves in the limestone and lava of the scattered islands of Melanesia. There are accounts of some caves in the Solomon Islands and New Caledonia whilst the Philippines have limestone which provided cave dwellings right up to the present time. Some American troops with spelunking interests found many possible 'leads' and, heading north towards Japan, the tiny island of Okinawa, which many know only from its wartime associations, is known to have over 200 caves including one called Gyokusen described as being 3 miles (over 5 kilometres) long.

Japan itself has a small but growing caving contingent

but little limestone of its own. What there is can be found on the main Honshu island in the Niigata Prefecture, nearly 200 miles (322 kilometres) north-west of Tokyo. The best known is the tourist cave of Akiyoshi-do some $6\frac{1}{4}$ miles (10 kilometres) in extent and which contends for a place among the world's most attractively adorned caverns. The deepest shaft was originally Omi-senri-do at 1353 feet (412 metres) but in 1976 another and deeper shaft, Byakuren-do, was explored to 1683 feet (512 metres).

I have had unconfirmed reports of caves on Taiwan (formerly Formosa) but on the South-East Asian landmass caves are known from the Malaysian peninsula, northwards up to Korea, Laos and into Burma. Many of them are known only as shrines such as the great temple at Batu, or interment sites preserved from further local exploration by superstitious fears. There are also reports of lava caves in South Korea where there has been some persistent exploration of passages up to 5 miles (8 kilometres) long.

China

Since the dramatic change in the attitude of the Chinese government to the outside world and the closer contacts made with the West, more has become known of the vast karst regions of that country. Sporting caving, as such, does not exist as yet but, as I write, there are possibilities of British speleologists penetrating the fantastically beautiful and only partially explored underworld. The caves of China range from the high mountains of the Himalayas down to the coastal regions. For the most part, the Chinese, as well as exploiting the beauty of their caves for cultural visits have had an intensely practical look at them as well. This stems, no doubt, from the thoughts of Chairman Mao Tse Tung who is quoted at the beginning of *Karst in China* as saying: 'Marxist philosophy holds that the most important problem does not lie in understanding the laws of the objective world and thus being able to explain it, but in applying the knowledge of these laws to change the world.' It is hard, in a caving context, to comprehend the intermingling of Mao, Marx and Frederick Engels but it probably explains why the Chinese could build a complete factory in a limestone cave with formations forming part of the backdrop to boilers and pipes or apply pure functionalism to cave waters for irrigation and hydro-electric power.

Provinces such as Kweichow, Kwangsi, Hunan, Hupeh, Kiangsu and Chekiang all have caverns of enviable size and adornment. Little is known as yet of lengths and depths of the Chinese systems but, in the realms of prehistory a great contribution was made in 1921 when excavation at Dragon Bone Hill cave at Choukoutien village in the Peking Province unearthed the bones of a Chinese ape-man. *Sinanthropus Pekinensis* (Peking Man) was a vital link in the evolutionary process of Man from the ape to *homo sapiens*. It is a miracle that this piece of evidence survived. Dragon Bone Hill cave got its name from the local belief that it

was the home of dragons long dead. It was mined for their bones which were pulverised for medicines and aphrodisiacs and no one knows how many Peking men and contemporaneous animal bones disappeared in this way. Once the scientific implications were realised, the study of this primitive forebear of Man intensified. Ironically, many of the preserved remains disappeared in another pulverisation – the bones of about forty individuals disappeared as they were being taken to the United States to be studied but never got there as total war came to the Pacific. Another interesting feature of China are the cave 'cities' carved in the loess plateau of Shanshi in the north. Loess is a lime-rich solidified sediment in which thousands of Chinese made their homes and is another aspect of the geological fascination of this country which has lived so long in isolation.

The USSR

Caves were known of throughout the Soviet Union for centuries, primarily as dwellings and holy places, but were used at various times to imprison political opponents or as catacombs. Soviet geologists have always taken an interest in their limestone area and had an early interest in the caves of the Crimea. But it was not until after the last war that speleology developed as a general activity. There are a great variety of caves in limestone and gypsum and, apart from the Crimea, the principal areas are the Caucasus, the Urals, the Altai-Sayanskaya, Pamyro-Tyang-Sryang, Turgai-Khazakhstan, central Siberia and Baikal-Stanovaya and the far east. As may be expected, speleology is now highly organised throughout the various States and several hundred caves and potholes have been explored and listed by the various official bodies, some of which rejoice under the title of 'Speleotourism'. The naming and codification of caves in any country is always difficult and whimsicality always creeps in. The Soviet Union is no exception, with such delights as Paryashchaya Ptitza (The Fleeting Bird) in the Bolshoi Caucasus. The deepest reported shaft system is the Kiewskaya in the Gissarsko-Altai, shown variously at 3117 feet (950 metres) and 3162 feet (964 metres). There is another unexplained 'depth record' of 3543 feet (1080 metres) in the Kilsi karst channel, presumably the same area as Kiewskaya. Nearly all the other deep ones are in the Bolshoi Caucasus (Kavkaz) between the Caspian and Black seas. From this region at the end of 1980 came news that the Russians were heading for a new depth record in the Snezhnaya (Snowy) Cave. A depth of 4200 feet (1280 metres) and a length of $5\frac{1}{2}$ miles (9 kilometres) was reported. The longest caves are in the Dnjepr-Black Sea karst region of the Ukraine, and the Optimisticheskaya is believed to be the longest in gypsum at Podolye. An official Soviet list has given it as 68 miles (109 kilometres) although it has in addition been reported to be 82 miles (131 kilometres). The cave is so convoluted, like many others in the region, that the full total of all the passages may never be known. The variety of caves includes lava tubes, ice caves (inevitably) and also (inevitably, but not in Siberia) the world's largest halite or rock salt cave in Tadzhikskaya near the Afghanistan border and not far from the Soviet Union's highest summit, Peak Communism (formerly Stalin Peak). This salt cave was reported at more than 3281 feet (1000 metres) long and 377 feet (115 metres) deep. As may be expected, cave exploration by foreigners is extremely difficult and my own overtures for permission to examine some of their caves and meet some of their speleological fraternity were unsuccessful even though I had made some good contacts among Soviet mountaineers.

Austria

Austria has one of the oldest caving traditions in Europe with a recorded exploration of the Drachenhol in the Steiermark province as far back as 1387. Organised caving began just over a hundred years ago with Franz Kraus. One of the country's deepest caves, the Lamprechtsofen, was explored as early as 1833 when evidence of a Bronze Age settlement was found. Lamprechtsofen is something like Castleguard in Canada – it is actually 'descended' by going up under the Leoganger Steinberg. In 1978 it was acclaimed as the highest cave in the world when Polish cavers made a tremendous breakthrough to achieve an interior distance of 3360 feet (1024 metres). As a result it shot up from forty-seventh in the world's depth league table to sixth with the prospect of achieving a possible 5905 feet (1800 metres). The country's deepest is the Schneeloch in the Tennengebirge not far from Salzburg. It has reached a depth of 3563 feet (1086 metres) following explorations by cavers from all over Europe and it could be extended in an upward direction as well. Recently, attention has been turned to the Dachstein *massif*, another big and complex area of limestone lying between the Tennengebirge and the Totes Gebirge. Naturally, as a mountainous country, Austria is also rich in ice caves and produced one of the earliest authorities on their structure and evolution, Professor Eberhard Fugger of Salzburg. Best known is the Eisreisenwelt in the Tennengebirge, which was first entered in 1879 by another early European speleologist, Anton von Posselt-Czorich. It is now fully exploited as a tourist attraction, a realm of perpetual glaciation adorned with ice formations irridescent with the colours from minerals seeping through in the water above. The Eisriesenwelt was also the scene of one of the first cave dives by Alexander von Mörk, a pioneer who, tragically, was killed in World War I. Had he survived he would have become one of the great names of speleology. His reinterred remains are part of a shrine in the cave.

Belgium

Belgium is alone among the Low Countries in possessing limestone caves of any note. The country has produced some fine speleologists, such as Professor Max Cosyns, who played such a part in the descent of the Pierre St Martin and the calm handling of the disaster when Marcel Loubens fell to his death. Belgium has two fine show caves in the Lesse valley on the edge of the Ardennes – the Rochefort and Han grottoes. The latter was known throughout Europe for centuries and there was a tentative exploration in 1771 by a local priest. A fuller exploration was not made until 1814 when four local men carrying torches made the first long penetration – and left a trail of flour on the floor to help them find their way back to the entrance.

Holland

There is no limestone in Holland capable of cave formation but the country does possess an interesting series of subterranean passages in the caves of Valkenburg. These are man-made through hundreds of years in the soft rock created by the impacting of the shells of bony sea-creatures millions of years ago. This labyrinth which goes on for miles has produced many finds of prehistoric interest.

France

France has always been the caving country *par excellence*. The range and variety of its caves and potholes seems unending, from the beautifully decorated passages of palaeolithic frescoes in the Dordogne and other areas to the deepest known caves in the world. I have enjoyed some of my happiest caving in that country in long, deep shafts, winding passages, great halls with huge formations, mysterious waterways, always with the possibility of finding something new. The caving regions, the most sporting ones anyway, stretch from the Franco-Spanish border and the Pyrénées, the high limestones on the fringe of the Alps and the central area in the Grands Causses, the Tarn gorges and the Dordogne. By chance, just after the last war I found myself in the valley of the river Cher and came upon Savonnières and was surprised to find the local caves were explored in 1547. France has always endeavoured to maintain its premier place with the world's deepest cave and did have the three deepest. But there are now seven European caves at least which have now passed the 1000 metre (3280 foot) mark and there are strong probabilities that there are deeper caves in some of the remote and higher mountain areas of the world where cave prospecting is still in its infancy.

For some years, two French caves have jockeyed for position for the honour of the deepest, the Gouffre Berger in the Sornin plateau above Grenoble, and the Pierre St Martin in the Pyrénées which actually passes under the French and Spanish border. The world's depth record was originally established in the Pierre St Martin in 1953 at 2388 feet (728 metres) but this was surpassed in the Gouffre Berger which in 1956 was the first to go beyond 1000 metres, being pushed to 3707 feet (1130 metres). Since then, the Pierre St Martin resumed its place at the top of the table at 4370 feet (1332 metres) for a short time. This was achieved by the simple expedient of finding an entrance higher up on the

90 (above) Immense stalagmites in the Gouffre Berger, France. *Tony Briggs*

91 (right) Straddling the Meanders, a winding cleft in the Gouffre Berger. *'Mif' Smith*

92 Lower exit of the Trou de Glaz in the dent de Crolles area of France.

Tête Sauvage. There was consternation in the caving world when the French electricity authority, which already had a hydro-electric station at the confluence of the streams from Larra and Saint Engrace, decided to burrow a tunnel which cut into the Pierre St Martin near its lowest point in the Salle Verna. The project was completed but its use was abandoned leaving a caving entrance which reduced the time to reach the actual bottom from hours to minutes. This quick way in has helped the exploration of the lower reaches and it could be that the Pierre St Martin may plunge even deeper.

The notion of starting higher up to get deeper down also caught on elsewhere. What was the second deepest cave in the world became top of the league with a depth of 4626 feet (1410 metres). It is likewise in a high mountain area; in fact the Jean-Bernard system, a fairly recent discovery near Samoens in the upper Giffre valley in the Haute Savoie, is within easy walking distance of Chamonix. The longest system in France honours the name of Félix Trombe, former President of the Spéléo Club de Paris, in the Arbas *massif* of the Haute Garonne. This complex of passages had a known length of 34 miles (54 kilometres) including some of the toughest caving pitches anywhere in the world. More diving is now going on in French caves than ever before, and areas which have hitherto attracted little attention, such as the rolling uplands of the Côte d'Or around Dijon, are full of promise. Apart from the obvious sporting appeal of these big systems, France has somewhere around a hundred caves of prehistoric importance with their primitive parietal art of early Man.

Germany

There is a great deal of limestone in Germany which is not immediately apparent as it lies in many places, under areas of vegetation. In a country of myths and legends, it is not surprising that caves were originally given a wide berth. But the practical demands for saltpetre, the *terre nitreuse* of the Middle Ages, compelled Hans Breu of Bayreuth to venture into the Ahornloch, now St Sophia's Cave. That was in 1490. Germany may also lay claim to the first recorded exploration of a cave listing the appropriate equipment used. This was the Breitwinner cave in the Fränkischer Jura and a pamphlet printed in 1535 indicates that the cavers from the town were by no means badly equipped even by modern standards, carrying with them lanterns, tinder-boxes, picks and ropes plus bread and wine. A year later, the country had its first show cave named after Friederich Baumann who found it, and which was later to inspire Geothe's poem *Winter journey in the Harz Mountains*. The Harz Mountains between the Leine and Elbe rivers, Sauerland and Swabian Franconian Jura provide the main caving areas. Most of the deepest shafts are in the Bayer Alps with Kargrabenhohl nearly 1476 feet (450 metres) having the greatest depth and the second deepest, the Salzgrabenhohle, being the longest with 4 miles (6½ kilometres) of passages. Germany's most famous cave

is the Schellenberg ice cavern in the Bavarian Unders-
berg mountains, listed with typical thoroughness on
the military maps as far back as 1826.

Greece

Greece and its caves are inevitably linked with its
ancient past, its caves being the haunt of deities,
oracles and the like. With his unerring instinct for
finding the right kind of cave environments throughout the European landmass, E.-A. Martel extended
his travels and recorded a visit to caverns in the
Peleponese limestone. In recent times French and
British cavers have probed the mountains of Arcadia
and the Pindus range. The first really deep shaft in
Greece, the Provatina, was found by Cambridge
University cavers near Ioannina (Yannina) in 1962. As
often happens, the local people swore it was bottomless
but eventually it was bottomed at 1329 feet (405
metres). It did not seem to go anywhere, but further
exploration of the area around Mount Astraka revealed
an even bigger gulf, the Epos Chasm, whose possibilities were first examined by two well-known British
cavers, Pete Livesey and Sion O'Neill. It turned out
that the Epos Chasm was later attacked by various
teams, and finally in 1979 the South Wales Caving
Club got down to 1490 feet (442 metres). Caves have
been investigated off the mainland in Corfu, Crete and
Kefallinia. At the latter, the island's principal town of
Argostolion has a mill with a unique source of power.
Its wheel is turned by sea water which then disappears
under the island and travels from west to east. It
debouches some 20 miles (32 kilometres) away on the
eastern side of the island, spurting back into the sea
from a resurgence about a metre higher than its
original sea-level entrance. A fascinating film has been
made of how cave divers solved the mystery of the
siphoning sea water. The phenomenon was eventually
proved to be due to the run-off water from the hills
above descending through the limestone, thereby
reducing the density of the sea water sufficiently for it
to rise. It also explains the mystery which has puzzled
people for centuries – fresh water sufficient to sustain
life rising from the sea-bed.

Italy

Italy closely rivals France for the numbers of cavers
and caves it possesses. The country once held the
world's depth record as far back as 1841 with 1086 feet
(331 metres) in the Grotta de Trebiciano in the Carso
Triestine. This area of limestone on the Italian-
Yugoslav border has been threatened with exploitation
which could ruin so many fine geological features.
British cavers have been extremely active in Italy. A
fellow townsman of mine, Stan Gee, has had a special
interest in the country's deepest, the Antro del Corchia
in the Appian Alps. This has a depth of 3117 feet (950
metres) but it is a system which has greater depth by
starting higher up. A new entrance, the Buca del
Cacciatori, is 1788 feet (545 metres) higher than the old
Antro entrance. Dye tests have led into the Corchia

93 Beginning the descent of the Spluga della Preta, near Verona, Italy.

system with the ultimate possibility of a depth of 4265
feet (1300 metres) being reached. In the era of modern
exploration the depth record was previously held by
the Spluga della Preta on the high, wind-blown
uplands above Verona, and was first British expedition
which I helped to film for the BBC in 1972. This is now
Italy's fourth deepest, at 2880 feet (878 metres) but,
like the Corchia, could come out lower down. British
cavers have also played a significant part in the
explorations of Italy's deepest cave, the Grotta di
Monte Cucco 3025 feet (922 metres) in the Umbrian
limestone. In the far west where the limestone merges
into the Alps Maritime in Piedmont, there has been
one of the most exciting discoveries, the beautiful cave
the Piagga Bella which has been explored to nearly 10
miles (16 kilometres) with a depth of 3000 feet (915
metres) and still going.

Norway

Norway is one of the loveliest countries in Europe and
not too overrun with tourists. British cavers are
extremely welcome over there, having helped to foster
the pastime among the local enthusiasts. Much of the

94 Cave country scenery in northern Italy near Spluga della Preta. In the background is the church of St Benedict in memory of Marisa Bolla Castellani and other cavers.

95 Crystalline roof in Trollkirke cave in Norway.

96 A typical British cavers' camp in Norway.

caving in Norway is within the Arctic Circle, wild, rugged landscape which is virtually unspoilt. Many of the caves are in pristine condition having been uncovered in the fairly recent geological past by the receding glaciers. The most usual starting point is Mo i Rana which sounds like a South Sea island but is a somewhat industrialised little town where the Norwegian caving organisation had its beginnings. One of the greatest problems in Norway is finding the cave entrances since they are often hidden away in the wilderness of forest and scrubland. Possibly the only disadvantage of caving in Norway is the mosquitoes and I once came across a somewhat bleary British expedition hiding in their tents using a noxious fumigant of their own concoction – they were smoking pipes with bits of carbide mixed in with the tobacco. There are now several hundred known and explored caves in the country and it was a British team, the Kendal Caving Club, which established the North European depth record in the Ragge-Javre-Raigegrotten. It was found above the isolated little Lapp settlement of Muskeen on the edge of the Hellemo fjord, an inaccessible spot reached only by boat or helicopter from Drag down the fjord. The Kendal cavers reached a depth of 1850 feet (564 metres) and it could go even lower. Further developments are always possible in Norwegian caves, such as the extension of the Greftvatn system at Gildeskål where Ulv and Arne Grønlie have been busy for some time. Also in the Salta area is Norway's longest cave, the Okshola-Kristihola, which is in excess of 4 miles (6

kilometres) and 525 feet (160 metres) deep. Beautiful little caves abound, such as the delightful Trollkirken, the Trolls' Church, north of Molde on the side of the Tverrfjella – well worth a visit in order to get off the beaten track.

Spain, Portugal and Gibraltar

There is one world-famous cave in Spain, at Altmira near Santillana de Mar, Santander, found by accident when a workman's dog fell into a hole in 1868. It later revealed a rich treasure house of Upper Palaeolithic cave art and bones. Tourist grottoes abound but serious caving has been going on in the vast areas of limestone which are still not fully explored. Spanish caving is well organised and well controlled. I suppose that Spain could lay claim to the deepest cave in the world as it had a share in the Pierre St Martin. Deepest in its own right is the Sima G.E.S. Malaga 3580 feet (1098 metres) in the Sierra de Tolox in southern Spain. The longest to date is the Ojo Guarena, 34 miles (55 kilometres) in the Corderilla Cantabrica near Burgos. Spain's own offshore islands also have caverns worth exploring, including far off Tenerife.

97 (overleaf, left) The Main Chamber of the Cueva de la Cotera, in the Cantabrian Mountains of northern Spain. In 1974 an expedition from Reading University Caving Club completed exploration of this cave. *Sheena Stoddard*

98 (overleaf, right) The Main Chamber of the Cueva Pimiango in the Cantabrian Mountains of northern Spain. Pimiango was explored and surveyed by a Kingswood caving group expedition in 1976. *Sheena Stoddard*

Neighbouring Portugal has a few caves in the Estremadura province near Porto de Moz. Gibraltar has little to appeal to the active caver but Old St Michael's Cave became, like so many other caves in populous areas, a concert hall.

Switzerland

This has always been more of a mountaineer's country than a potholer's but what there is of its underworld is well worth exploring. It only has one cave on a grand scale, but what a scale it is! The Hölloch (Hell Hole) lies appropriately at the very heart of Switzerland and from whence it derived its name, Schwytz in the Muotatal. It is second only to the Flint-Mammoth system and Alois Ulrich little knew that when he first entered its portal in 1875, the underground passages would eventually be explored for 84 miles (135 kilometres). Superbly decorated in places, dank and drab in others, there have been times when it has lived up to its title of Hell Hole. No one had really seen the water passages in such spate until 1952 when it trapped a party led by the redoubtable Professor Alfred Bögli, a leading authority on the cave. They were cut off for ten days – with only rations for one day. He told me afterwards that there was so much water that his little group were resigning themselves to try and survive for three weeks. The Hölloch has the distinction of being Switzerland's deepest as well at 2717 feet (828 metres). Swiss cavers, however, have been looking further afield. I once spent a poor Alpine season pottering round the limestone about Interlaken and recent events have confirmed my impression that there was more to go at than the Hölloch. The area around Habkern near the easy Augstmatthorn and Beatenberg on the Güggisgrat have yielded hidden depths. The Siebenhengste complex has been plumbed to 2677 feet (816 metres) and is 22 miles (35 kilometres) long with flood passages indicating that more lies beyond.

Yugoslavia

The Yugoslav word *kras* translated into *karst* in German is the definitive description for the limestone which has special interest to speleologists. It was originally applied to the dry, limestone uplands of the Dinaric Alps along the Yugoslavian Adriatic seaboard, a 400 mile (640 kilometre) range linked by the Julian Alps in the north to the main Alpine system. The Julian Alps have magnificent mountain scenery culminating in the limestone peak of Triglav 9395 feet (2864 metres). With so much limestone, it was inevitable that Yugoslavia should become prominent in the study of this form of geology. Long before the birth of modern Yugoslavia either as a monarchy or a republic, the Slovenian scientist Ivan Valvassor wandering among the *poljes* and mountain regions of the country, described some seventy caves. He was the first to describe the cave salamander (*proteus*) in 1689. The first caves to be explored were at what was once Adelsberg in the old Hapsburg Empire and now better known as Postojna which now has one of the world's leading karst research institutions. The caves of Postojna and Skocijan are best known for their public show facilities. The former has a true length of 8 miles (13 kilometres) and has a small gauge electric railway as one of its attractions. The Krizna Jama (Cross Cave) has some superb subterannean lake scenery where underground boating comes into its own, with so many lakes to be traversed. The underground waters of the Pivka river, the Rijeka and the Malensca are still a fascinating study in themselves. The Rijeka travels some 21 miles (33 kilometres) before emerging into daylight in the Timavo springs in Italy. Yugoslavia's deepest cave was the Pološka Jama at 2247 feet (684 metres) near Tolomin in the Julian Alps in Slovenia. This has since been surpassed by the Brezno Pri Gamsori Glavici, also in the Julian Alps.

East Europe

Czechoslovakia, Hungary and Poland are Eastern bloc countries with growing caving popularity. Like France and Spain sharing the depths of the Pierre St Martin, Czechoslovakia and Hungary have a mutual interest in their biggest system, the Domica-Baradla. The whole length meandering under the frontier is some 16 miles (25 kilometres), with Hungary claiming the longest section. One of Czechoslovakia's longest caves and one of the first to be scientifically explored is the Mococha in the Moravian karst, described by the mathematician Nagel in 1748. The country's longest, Demänovska, 13 miles (21 kilometres) in a deep valley of the Nizke Tatry or Low Tatra, was known about even before that date. The deepest is also in the Low Tatra, Jaskyna Zaskocie at 889 feet (271 metres). Hungary's deepest, like the Baradla system, is near the village of Aggtelek. The Vesembükki Zsomboly has been explored to 804 feet (245 metres). Poland has fairly extensive caving areas in the Tatra on Czechoslovakia's northern border and the Cracovian Jura. Scientific exploration of the caves around Ojcow revealed mammoth remains and the country claims Eastern Europe's deepest shaft, the Jaskini Snieznej, which ends in a siphon at 2569 feet (783 metres). Once a mere 460 feet (140 metres) the Mietusia, also in the Tatra, has been explored for 5 miles (8 kilometres). In addition to several hundred caves, the country is renowned for its halite or salt mines at Wiliczka whose galleries are reputed to extend for over 200 miles (322 kilometres).

Romania is associated with one of the greatest names in scientific caving, the eminent naturalist Emile Racowiza. He was among the first to systematise cave exploration which paved the way to such underground laboratories as the Grotte de Moulis in the Pyrénées. Many of Romania's known caves are in the Bihorrului mountain region not far from where Racowiza established himself in the chair of geology at Cluj (Kolozvar) University. The small but growing band of Romanian cavers reached a depth of 1362 feet (415 metres) in the Pestera Tausoare and their longest, Pestera Vintului, has reached 13 miles (22 kilometres) and also makes a gradual ascent inside the mountain.

The growing significance of caving in Bulgaria was reflected in 1980 in the choice of Sofia for the European speleological conference to exchange information about karst research, especially in that country and throughout the Balkans. Sofia is not far from Pernik (Dimitrovo) on the northern end of the Rila Planina where the longest cave, Douchlata, has been explored for 7 miles (11 kilometres). The deepest shaft has been listed as the Raytchova Doupka, 1220 feet (372 metres) at Lovech on the northern edge of the Stara Planina.

Asia Minor and the Middle East
The remote areas of Turkey contain limestone and a lava belt with a weird geology of its own. To arrive at Urgub in Anatolia unprepared is to receive a shock at the sight of such a profusion of shelters, caves and grotesque shapes which suggest a lunar landscape. In southern Turkey, the Taurus mountains, the Toros Dagi, have limestone which gives characteristic shape to some of the uplands and are one of the most promising areas for medium-distance expeditions. British cavers along with members of the Spéléo Club de Paris have been the most active and dye tests to help the Turkish government with dam-building operations and water sources have revealed a large area with caving possibilities. Britons Tony Dunford and John Middleton helped to find Turkey's known deepest, the Düdencik at Cevizli with a recorded depth of 1082 feet (330 metres), during the hydrological study for the Manavgat hydro-electric project. In the same area the resurgence cave Pinar Gözü was examined for a few thousand feet. I have found the possibility of a number of caves in the Rize mountains in north-east Turkey where the karst country seems to be linking up with the Bolshoi Caucasus just beyond, in the Soviet Union. More recently, another caving area in Turkey has been found near the Black Sea coast near the coal mining town and provincial capitol of Zonguldak. This area and another further south at Safranbolu have been explored by British teams and further prospects are good.

Iran has always had a number of caves of historic interest and when I was in Fars, the home province of Persia, as it formerly was, I had a look at the impressive cave near Kazeroon with its huge statue of Shapur, the Sassanian king. Other historic caves include the Moghan grotto in Khorosan and the caves at Rud-Afshare, Kanak and Yakh-Morad nearer to Tehran. These have no great penetration, but the intense geological probing caused by the need for oil revealed that the country has some extremely large areas of limestone mainly in the south-west where the Zagros mountains reach to a height of nearly 15,000 feet (4572 metres) stretching from Kurdistan with spurs into Fars and Bahktiari and down into Baluchistan. The Zagros has seen some intense caving activity since the 1970s, especially by British and French teams. One of the outstanding expeditions of modern times in the caving world was that of 1972 to Ghar Parau. Led by the distinguished caver David Judson it sought to follow up the exploration of the previous year led by John Middleton who was the inspiration of the concept of deep caves in the Zagros limestone. It was hoped that Ghar Parau with its huge shafts would have achieved the world's depth record, the equivalent of finding and conquering another Everest. Alas, it was not to be, despite the brilliantly planned and executed expedition in this isolated part of the world. Ghar Parau now stands at 2464 feet (751 metres) and has something over a kilometre of passages. A further depth record attempt was made in 1977 with a team including divers. It sought to follow up the prospecting by the French around the Antenna Ridge of Kuh-e-Shahu. In the end it revealed only tantalising possibilities and a growing awareness that, but for the various troubles, Iran could be the country most likely to produce some sensational caving news in the 1980s.

Between the Mediterranean and the Persian Gulf, geological maps reveal areas of limestone but most of it is unexplored from a caving point of view. Israel has many natural caves as well as those man-made associated with the early days of Christianity. The Lebanese range of mountains, which reach up to 10,000 feet (3048 metres) have masses of chalk and limestone in their structure which possibly accounts for the meaning of the country's name, The White One. The oldest known cave in the range is linked with mythical legend for it is the birthplace of the Adonis river which gushes from deep underground at Afka. The myth has it that it was here that the love goddess Astarte met Adonis for the first time and where the Adonis flower, the red anemone which sprang from his blood after he had been killed by a boar, is a sight to behold. The river has provided vital water and power for communities along its banks for generations. Jeïta cave is probably the best known in the Middle East and is now a show cave. It extends for over 5 miles (8 kilometres) and is spectacularly decorated and dramatic with a strongly flowing river. Not far from the main road from Beirut to Damascus which winds over the extensive limestone plateau are probably scores of shafts awaiting discovery. Some have been visited by British cavers and the Spéléo Club du Liban which has made an intensive reconnaissance of the country's backbone. Shafts of considerable depth have been descended including the deepest, Faouar Dara, explored to 2041 feet (622 metres) which is one of the most exciting descents in the world.

India and the Himalayas
There are varying accounts of how much or how little limestone is known throughout the Indian continent. The best known caves are mostly man-made and associated with the religions of the country. The temple caves at Ellora in the Aurangbad district of Bombay extend along 1½ miles (2½ kilometres) of cliff; the caves on Elephanta Island go back to the third

century whilst the Ajanta caves along the ravine of the river Wagura north-east of Ellora date back to 200 BC. The real caving possibilities lie well to the north where travellers, like myself, have often been struck by the appearance of limestone and great height. Some of the mountain villages I have visited are almost duplicates of the grey-white villages of our British caving areas. The prevalence of goitre among the hill people due to drinking water deficient in iodine has been noted before. In terms of geological time, the Himalayas are extremely young. Everest is a young mountain almost within the time scale of man himself and limestone surges up through many parts of this great mountain chain. Millions of years ago seas must have covered this region creating the limestone which was thrust up later. Unfortunately, the rainfall, so necessary for cave formation, is almost non-existent in the realms of eternal snow. Yet the *Rig-Veda* contains a poem which refers to Indra, the Hindu god, releasing seven rivers 'from the cave's depths' in these mountains. A British karst research expedition to Kashmir found a good deal of non-caveable limestone and it is Nanga Parbat, 26,629 feet (8117 metres) to the north which holds the record for the world's highest known cave, a small, ice-encrusted passage at 21,653 feet (6600 metres) on Rakhiot Peak.

When I was on the Nuptse expedition I found a cave which, from a distance, looked like Ossian's cave in Glencoe. It was impossible to reach, so that I could gain no estimate of its length and I put its height at about 22,000 feet (6705 metres) but I had no means of measuring it accurately. Nepal has a number of caves lower down, especially around Pokhara in the west. One became very popular when it was visited by the late King Mahendra and the most exciting is the Harpan River Cave which has an impressive entrance with a big waterfall and the lower reaches almost completely submerged. The Plain of Pokhara is about 3000 feet (915 metres) high spread over 150 square miles (388 square kilometres) and, with its rainfall, has excellent prospects for cave exploration. Ironically, further to the north, tower the icy summits of Dhaulagiri, 26,795 feet (8167 metres) and Annapurna 26,492 feet (8075 metres) on each side of the Kali Gandaki. It was here that the British karst research team made the most important discovery of all – the world's highest and thickest block of limestone. Its thickness was measured as 15,420 feet (4700 metres), nearly as high as Mont Blanc. Like that other area of great thickness in Kashmir, it is, as yet, without caves or even slight indentations. It will need a complete climatic change and the penetrating power of rainwater to carve passages in this solid mass. Who knows, it may prove to be the ultimate challenge for cavers many thousands of years from now.

Africa

This vast continent is still one of the great enigmas of the caving world. The extent of its limestone is only partially known and there are caves in sandstone and lava. Limestone is the thickest and most plentiful in the north and southern regions where Europeans with a caving background in the days of colonialism did most of the searching for shafts. Africa possesses some of the finest cave art and there are strong arguments that in the dim past there was an ethnic link between the cave dwellers of Europe and those of the dark continent. Negroid man is known to have existed in Europe. The limestone in greatest abundance lies in the north-west in Morocco, Algeria and Tunisia, with possible links with the karst on the other side of the Mediterranean. A number of caves have been explored in the remote – and even now, little explored – Atlas mountains. Algeria can claim the deepest, the Anou Boussoill, south of Tizi Ouzou in the hills of Djurdjura. First discovered by two French alpinists in 1937 it had desultory explorations which are still going on. A depth of 1657 feet (505 metres) has been recorded and the caving world awaits with interest the findings of the Polish expedition which went there in 1979. Further west in Morocco the Toghobeit cave has been extended from 1837 feet (560 metres) to 2296 feet (700 metres). This area of the Atlas mountains east of Rabat should yield more in time. Tunisia has less to offer; although the limestone breaks out in the Aures *massif*, no caves of any great depth or length have yet been found; the deepest known being the Djebel Serdj, some 5577 feet (1700 metres) long and 876 feet (267 metres) deep. Right in the middle of the Sahara in south Algeria in the Ahaggar (Hoggar) mountains is a world of upthrust lava peaks in a desolate landscape, having links with man's primitive past in the caves of Tassili-n-Ajer. The paintings of lions, elephants and giraffes suggest that this heartland of the Sahara had a different – and wetter – climate than today.

Caves have been found further over in the north-east in Ethiopia east of Addis Ababa, some with active river passages like the Webbe at Sof Omar. One of the deepest potholes is in the Antalo limestone near Bedenno. Now known as the Enkoftu Mohu, I last heard of it having a depth of nearly 650 feet (200 metres) and it is richly adorned with flowstone and other formations. There is also a literary curiosity associated with Ethiopia and caves. The mountains include Mount Amara, reputedly the Mount Abora of Coleridge's poem Kubla Khan and Xanadu.

Where Alph, the sacred river, ran
Through caverns measureless to man
Down to a sunless sea.

By what process, I wonder, did Coleridge's dream transport him so accurately to a river passage in old Abyssinia if not by opium?

Deeper south are the volcanic regions of Kenya and a considerable number of lava caves including one I have previously mentioned, Leviathan, believed to be the world's longest in the Chyulu Range. It is 150 miles (240 kilometres) from Nairobi, the base of the Cave

Exploration Group of East Africa which has undertaken a great deal of exploratory work in this area. At the last count Leviathan was 7 miles (11 kilometres) long with a depth of 1541 feet (470 metres). There are also volcanic masses in the Cameroons; Gabon and the Congo are known to have limestone which has had a few visits from the colonising Europeans. In the south-west of Africa there have been a few deep penetrations. The Cango caves near Oudtshoorn in South Africa are now show caves with some fine formations. Some caves, alas, have been used as glorified dustbins used to absorb the detritus from mining operations. The only deep cave at West Dreifontein was threatened in this way. The Drakensberg should also have some lava caves in its 700 mile (1126 kilometre) length. The sandstone caves found in this range have revealed evidence of their inhabitation by the earliest bushmen on this continent. Off the coast of Mozambique, the island of Madagascar, now the Malagasy Republic, has an extensive limestone region in the Maramokotro *massif* in the north-east of the island near Ambilobe. There is more in the high plateaux of the south but, for many reasons, including its remoteness, it has had scant expedition attention.

APPENDIX 1
CAVE PRESERVATION CODE

1 Cavers, like all other people who go out of doors, should have the goodwill of the farmers and country communities at heart. Care should be taken to obtain permission to cross private land and cavers should co-operate with farmers, landowners and their agents, because thoughtless actions by cavers prevent other parties from enjoying the pleasures of underground exploration. Cavers should uphold the Countryside Code and guard against risk of fires, fasten all gates through which they pass, keep dogs (if they have them) under control and keep to the paths across farmland. It is important not to trample on growing crops. It should be remembered, too, that grass is also a valuable growing crop and cannot be cut by machinery if flattened. Avoid damaging fences, hedges and walls.

2 Make no excavations or diversions of water without permission. If fluorescein or other chemicals are to be used, check if it is going to go into the drinking water of a farm or a village community. Warn people in advance of its use and stress they are quite harmless. If excavations or diversions of water are made seek permission and make sure that adequate care is taken to prevent animals and people from falling in.

3 Respect the other cavers' digs and explorations, pay such dues as may be required, get such permits as are required and return keys when finished with.

4 Choose a route carefully and make no additional tracks unless it is absolutely necessary.

5 Discourage solo descents and ensure that members of your group are properly trained.

6 Use adequate lighting so that fragile formations and other interesting features of the underworld, particularly the crystalline floors and roof formations, are not disfigured with mud or destroyed by your colliding with them.

7 Be careful when taking photographs, especially on rare occasions when using flash powder which has explosive qualities and can damage delicate formations. Remove your spent flash bulbs and cartons.

8 Leave stalactites, stalagmites, helictites, flowstone and rimstone pools as clean and undamaged as when they were found. Do not trespass across sections taped off to conserve formations.

9 Commit no acts of vandalism by breaking off portions of formations to take out as souvenirs. Remember other people want to see them *in situ*.

10 Never disfigure the walls of a cave by writing or drawing on them. Stop people from blackening their initials on cave walls with carbide lights or candles. If a record must be left of your depth in a cave, use metal club tags and leave them.

11 Try to leave the natural life of a cave as undisturbed as possible. If specimens are required take only enough for identification.

12 Do not disturb the evidence of floods or other episodes in the cave's history.

13 Remember that caves can be fouled by insanitary habits and, if vital natural functions have to be carried out, select a spot away from running water and the natural passage of cavers.

14 Treat the cave as a Nature Reserve. Leave the cave and its contents in the condition you would expect to find it. Leave no litter. If you find any, take it out with you.

15 Avoid polluting the water by various means. Take out your spent carbide, which is poisonous, and batteries.

16 If there are signs of human or animal occupation do not disturb them until they can be examined by experts.

17 Let someone small tackle the exploration of a passage where formations might be damaged.

18 If it is necessary to drain pools, use wherever possible the siphoning method, so as not to upset the natural conditions of a cave. Avoid, if possible, permanently withdrawing water from a part of the system as this can upset the natural balance of a cave.

19 Be courteous and helpful when dealing with newspaper, television and broadcasting reporters. Remember they have a job to do and require only the facts for their reports.

APPENDIX 2
NATIONAL AND INTERNATIONAL CAVING ORGANISATIONS

THE BRITISH ISLES
British Association of Caving Instructors
Hon. Secretary, Coronet House, Queen Street, Leeds LS1 4PW.

British Cave Research Association
Secretary Ian G. Penney, 9 Grandview Road, Thundersley, Essex SS7 3JZ.

Cave Diving Group
Martin Bishop, Bishop's Cottage, The Batch, Priddy near Wells, Somerset BA5 3BD.

Cave Rescue Council
Secretary Eric Catherine, 4 Christine Close, Ash, Aldershot, Hants GU12 6OL.

Council of Northern Caving Clubs
Secretary Brian Smith, 15 North Street, Idle, Bradford BD10 0RP.

Council of Southern Caving Clubs
Secretary Fred Davies, Camp 5, Neighbourne, Oakhill, Somerset.

Derbyshire Caving Association
Secretary Mrs Jenny Potts, 3 Greenway, Hulland Ward, Derby DE6 3FE.

National Caving Association
c/o Geography Department, University of Birmingham, Box 363, Birmingham 15.

Subterranea Britannica
Secretary Elaine Blatchford, 21 Briary Lane, Royston.

Whernside Manor Cave & Fell Centre
The Warden, Whernside Manor, Dent, Sedbergh, Cumbria.

William Pengelly Cave Studies Trust
Buckfastleigh, Devon. Secretary J. Wilmut, 80 De Beauvoir Road, Reading, Berks.

Cambrian Caving Council – Cyngor Ogofeydd Cymreig
Secretary Frank Baguley, 15 Elm Grove, Gadlys, Aberdare, Mid-Glam 8DN CF44.

Scottish Caving Council
Grampian Speleological Group, 8 Scone Gardens, Edinburgh EH8 7DQ.

Irish Speleological Association
c/o Department of Geography, Trinity College, Dublin 2.

Speleological Union of Ireland
1 Sweetmans Avenue, Blackrock, Co. Dublin.

AUSTRALIA   Australian Speleological Federation
123 Manningham Street, Parkville, Victoria 3052.

AUSTRIA   Verband Osterreichischer Hohlenforscher
Obere Donaustrasse 99-7-3, A-1020 Wien.

BELGIUM   Fédération Nationale de Spéléologie et Alpinisme
rue Gillaux 14, B-4900, Angleur, Liége.
Comité National Belge de Spéléologie
avenue des Paradisiers 66, B1060 Bruxelles.
Fédération Spéléologie
avenue Michel Ange 49, B1040 Bruxelles.

BRAZIL   Sociedade Brasileira de Speleologie
Rua 24 de Maio, C62 cj465, Caixa Postal 7820, Sao Paolo.

BULGARIA   Fédération Bulgare de Spéléologie
Boul. Skobelev 7, BG 1463 Sofia.

CANADA   Société Québéçois de Spélélologie
1415 est, rue Jarry, Montreal, Quebec province H2E 2Z7.

FRANCE   Fédération Française de Spéléologie
130 rue St Maur, F-75011 Paris.

GREECE   Société Spéléologie de Grèce
11 rue Mantzarou, Athens 135.

ITALY   Societa Speleologica Italiana
c/o Frazz. tuffo 14023, Cocconate, Asti.
Commissione Centrale per la Speleologia
via Ugo Fescolo 3, 20121 Milan.

LUXEMBOURG   Groupe Spéléologique Luxembourgeois

MEXICO   Groupp Espeleologico Mexicano
Salonica No. 233, Mexico 16, DC.

NORWAY   Norwegian Caving Association
c/o Postbox 225 Mo i Rana.

POLAND   Fédération Polonaise d'Alpinisme
ul Sienkiewicza 12/439, Pl – 100 010 Warsaw.

PORTUGAL   Sociedide Portuguesa de Espeleologia
Rue Saraiva de Carvalho 233, Lisbon 3.

ROMANIA   Institutoal de Spelologie E.C. Racovita
Stra. Mihail Moxa 9, R-7000, Bucarest 12.

SWEDEN   Sveriges Speolog – Förbund
Fack 102 60, Stockholm 4.

SOUTH AFRICA South African Spelaeological Society
PO Box 4812, Cape Town.

TURKEY   Société Spéléologique de Turquie
PK 229, Bakanliklar, Ankara.

UNITED STATES   National Speleological Society, Inc.
Cave Avenue, Huntsville, Alabama 35810.

YUGOSLAVIA   Institute for Karst Research
67230 Postojna, Titov trg 2.

Speleological Section Zeljezničar Mountaineering Club
410000 Zagreb, Trnjanska 5b.

CAVE RESCUE ORGANISATIONS

Derbyshire
Call Derbyshire County police HQ, tel. Ripley 3551; Bill Whitehouse, Clovelly Cottage, Lower Terrace Road, Tideswell, Derbyshire. Tel. Tideswell 661 (home), Matlock 2304 (office).

Devon
Call Devon and Cornwall police HQ, tel. Exeter 67444.

Gloucester
Call Gloucester police, tel. Cheltenham 21321; P.W. Taylor, 7 Ogbourne Close, Longlevens, Gloucester GL2 OHW. Tel. Gloucester 28908.

Mendip
Call Somerset and Avon police via 999; Jim Hanwell, 50 Wells Road, Wookey Hole, Wells, Somerset BA5 1DN.

South East
Call Metropolitan police or county police for appropriate area or dial 999; Eric Catherine, 4 Christine Close, Ash, Aldershot, Hants GU12 6QL. Tel. Aldershot 20921 (home), Camberley 65222 (office).

Upper Wharfedale
Call police at Grassington, tel. Grassington 752222 or Skipton 3377.

Yorkshire
Call police at Settle, tel. Settle 2542/2543; Bob Hart, The Green, Rathmell, Settle, N. Yorkshire, BD24 OJX. Tel. Settle 3614.

Ireland
Call police at Belfast, tel. Belfast 605222. Gardai, Dublin, Dublin 77156; Maurice Neill, 53 Rosscoole Park, Belfast. Tel. Belfast 773068.

Scotland
Call Edinburgh police, tel. Edinburgh 1212.

North Wales
Call north Wales police, tel. Colwyn Bay 57171; John Needham, 29 Greenfields, Upton by Chester.

South Wales
Call Bridgend police, tel. Bridgend 2444, Abercrave 613 or John Barrows, Abercrave 283; Bob Hall, Flat 1, 17 High Street, Newport, Salop. Tel. Newport 810565 (work).

Abseil A method of roping down a pitch instead of using a ladder. Also known as a rappel.

Acetyline See **Carbide**.

Active system A cave system which is still in the course of formation.

Adit A word used in lead-mining to indicate a level or sloping entrance to a mine. Often a drainage tunnel from a mine.

Affluent A tributary system of a river, stream or lake.

Afflux The upstream rise of water level above normal surface of water in a channel or passage due to contraction or obstruction of the normal waterway.

Afterglow The fluorescent reaction of some formations which glow, usually green, after a strong light such as a flash bulb or torch is shone on them. An indication of a younger formation.

Albinism Animals, fish, plants and insects lacking normal colouration due to deprivation of sunlight.

Alluvium Finely grained silty material deposited by a river or stream.

Ameliorite A form of crystalline stalagmite more popularly called cave flowers.

Anastomosis A branching network, like arteries, of tubular channels in limestone, usually in bedding planes, rarely in joint planes.

Anemolite A stalactite (often called a helictite) which forms contrary to gravity and, as its name indicates, is formed by the passage of air or wind curving it away from the vertical.

Anthodite Another form of cave flower formed from long, fine crystals of gypsum or aragonite.

Aquifer A belt of waterlogged permeable rocks.

Aragonite Calcium carbonate in crystalline form. It is slightly heavier than calcite.

Ascenders See **Prusik**.

Aven A shaft in the roof of a cave leading to an upper passage.

Beck An old Norse word often used in Yorkshire and the Lake District for stream.

Beck head The emergence of a stream at its exit point from underground.

Bed A layer, deposit or stratum of rock, usually in a belt of sedimentary rock.

Bedding cave A cave formed by the erosion of a bedding plane – usually low and wide.

Bedding (or stratification) plane The separating point between one stratum of rock and another.

Bedrock The ultimate rock on which alluvial or detrital material rests.

Belay A point to which ladders or rope anchorages can be fixed. Also the use of ropes for the protection of cavers and climbers.

Blende Zinc sulphide, sometimes known as sphalerite, zinc blende or Black Jack. Occurs with galena in various deposits, and replaces calcite in limestones.

Blowhole Sometimes known as a gloop – a small hole in the floor or ceiling of a cave through which a draught is detected. More usual in sea caves.

Blue John Fluorspar, fluorite or Derbyshire spar. Calcium fluoride found mainly in Derbyshire where it is worked ornamentally; formerly as the flux in the steel trade.

Bone cave A cave in which bones, usually prehistoric, have been found.

Bore A fast-flowing river with great erosive power due to its speed and the chiselling effect of stones carried in it.

Bore hole A hole bored by the pressure of water. A hole bored in the floor of a cave to take samples or detect a further cave or passage beneath.

Boss A short, stubby, rounded stalagmite.

Boulder choke A blockage caused by rock fall from roof to ceiling.

Boulder clay (or till) A clayey deposit containing stones and erratic boulder.

Bowline A knot used for belaying.

Brachiopod A fossilised shellfish known as a lampshell found in carboniferous limestone.

Breccia A group of rocks consisting of angular fragments. They may be formed by crushing or faulting, volcanism or erosion. Cave breccia often includes fossil bones.

Bridge A rock arch, or a rock wedged across a passage. Also a technique of climbing by spanning a crack or chimney.

Cache A storage place for provisions for exploration and emergency.

Calcareous Containing, or formed from, calcite.

Calcite Calcium carbonate $CaCO_3$. White to yellowish in colour – the main constituent of limestone and cave formations.

Canal A cave passage of still or static water, or a mine passage.

Capillary action The movement of water in the interstices of rock due to capillary forces.

Capillary fringe The zone immediately above the water table containing capillary water.

Carbide Calcium carbide mixed with water to produce acetyline gas in carbide lamps used for caving.

Carboniferous A geological period in which the lower carboniferous limestones were laid down.

Cascade Calcite formation which has coated rocks and looks like a 'frozen' waterfall.

Cat hole A very tight squeeze through a very small crack or hole in the rock.

Cat-run (or -walk) A fairly low crawl.

Cave Any underground hollow or natural cavity travelling in a horizontal direction. A cave may lead to a pothole – a pothole may include a cave system. Usually a system which does not require the use of ladders and ropes to explore.

Cave art Paintings, engravings, statues made by Palaeolithic Man.

Cave deposit The debris on the floor of a cave consisting of clay, silt, gravel, residue of formations.

Cave of debouchure A cave entered at the opposite end from which a stream enters.

Cave pearl A round piece of calcite formation resembling a real pearl created by being rotated by water action in a pool.

Cave system The whole complex of interlinking passages underground.

Caver A cave explorer or speleologist.

Cavern Generally taken to mean a large underground cave or system.

Cavernicolous A form of life which fulfils its complete cycle underground.

Cavernophilous Forms of life which exist temporarily underground.

Cenote Mexican term for a pothole with a permanent depth of water or lake in the system.

Cerussite White lead ore and often associated with galena.

Chamber A large cavern.

Chert Beds and nodular concretions in limestone.

Chimney A narrow, vertical fissure climbed by jamming.

Chockstone A rock wedged in a narrow cleft, sometimes used as a belay point.

Choke A blockage of a passage, chimney or pothole by rocks, clay, silt, etc.

Claustrophobia A morbid fear of enclosed spaces.

Clinometer An instrument for measuring the dip of a stratum or a fault.

Clints Fretting of surface limestone blocks caused by corrosive action.

Column A stalactite and stalagmite which have bonded to form a pillar.

Conglomerate A consolidated rock composed of gravel or pebbly deposits.

Controlled entry A system of allowing access to caves only with permission by barring the way in with lids, doors and locks.

Corrasion The abrasion of a stream passage by rock held in suspension in water.

Corrosion The chemical work performed by water containing carbon dioxide in eroding rock.

Crack A small fissure.

Crawl A low passage along which it is possible to proceed only on hands and knees.

Crinoidea The most familiar fossils in limestone; sometimes stone lilies.

Cross fault A subsidiary fault, almost at right angles to a main fault.

Crystal pool A pool with little or no overflow which contains crystal deposits.

Current marks Referred to variously as scalloping or fluting. Marks caused by water power rushing against the rock.

Curtain Sometimes refers to a row of stalactites hanging down in a horizontal line. More usually it means a thin sheet of formation (streaky bacon) hanging down from the roof of a cave.

Dark zone That part of a cave which is beyond the limit of daylight.

Deads Barren veins of rock. Often used by miners of old to build protective walls.

Debouchure The resurgence point of an underground stream where it emerges from the cave mouth.

Descenders Various mechanical frictional devices for controlling descent.

Detritus Rock, sand or gravel deposit formed by river action.

Dig A place where a cave explorer digs to remove a blockage to further exploration or to find a new cave.

Dip The angle of inclination of a bed of rock from the horizontal, indicated in degrees.

Distributary A branch of a stream flowing from the main stream but not rejoining it again.

Dog tooth crystal A variety of calcite with crystals showing a combination of scalenohedral and prism.

Doline Surface depressions caused by the collapse of large caves below.

Dolomite Calcium and magnesium carbonate ($CaCO_3$, $MgCO_3$). Occurs in widespread sedimentary beds. Named after the French deologist, Dolomieu.

Drag stretcher A specially designed stretcher made for cave rescue. It has eyelets and attachments for dragging in low crawls and is usually made from rubber.

Drainage level A level tunnel driven by miners to drain a mine.

Drapery Curtain formation which is in waves or folds.

Dripstone A general word for formations caused by falling water with chemical in suspension.

Dry suit Thermally insulated waterproof diving suit, i.e. worn over suitable underwear.

Duck A point where the roof of a cave meets the water level and can be traversed by a quick swim on lung power or by ducking under and coming up at the other side. Often misnamed a siphon. Cave divers also refer to a duck where there is a minimal air space and they must traverse completely submerged.

Ebbing and flowing pools Pools where water rises and falls rhythmically, possibly by syphonic action.

Effluent cave Cave of debouchure.

Electron ladder A ladder made of wire with metal rungs, light to carry, easy to instal and eliminating the use of moisture-holding rope ladders.

Encrustation A crust of formation covering anything in a cave.

Entomology The study of insects.

Erosion The wearing away of rocks by chemical or other physical means.

Exposure The deterioration of a body due to wet, cold and inadequate amount of food and liquid. Also used to refer to the steepness of a rock pitch and the depth one could fall.

Exposure suit Specially designed clothing to keep a body warm and dry and to combat cold in adverse cave conditions.

Eye splice A loop made on the ends of electron ladders to facilitate clipping to further sections and belay points.

Fault A fracture in the rocks or Earth's crust displacing one side relative to the other.

Fissure An extensive open fracture in limestone.

Film water Thin covering of water moving slowly over walls and formations.

Firing Exploding a charge to loosen rock.

Flattener A low crawl in a bedding plane.

Flowstone A continuous covering of calcite on a floor or wall.

Fluorescein A powerful, harmless dye used for tracing the underground flow of water and its emergence points.

Fluorspar See **Blue John**.

Fluting Sharp-edged groove or channel.

Formation Generally, all forms of calcareous deposits in caves creating the various shapes, and also takes in aragonite and gypsum.

Fossils The preserved remains of life from previous geological ages.

Free-dive Using one's own lung power and no apparatus to get through a siphon or flooded passage.

Galena Lead sulphide. An important source of lead. Extensively mined in limestone and sandstone.

Gallery A high-level cave passage linking one part of the system with another part of the main system.

Ginging Lining a lead mine or other shaft to prevent the sides caving in.

Gloop See **Blowhole**.

Gour A rimstone pool.

Grike The fissure created in clints by the solution of rock in the joints.

Ground water Water below the water table.

Grotto A picturesque cave, usually lit up in show caverns.

Guano Excreta of bats or birds deposited in cave sites.

Gypsum Hydrated calcium sulphate ($CaSO_4.2H_2o$).

Hade The angle made by a fault or fissure in relation to the vertical. See also **Dip**.

Harness Systems of webbing tape to be worn round the seat or chest for attachment to abseil and prusik equipment.

Header Top extension of a ladder used for joining to another section, or securing at the head of a pitch.

Helictite See **Anemolite**.

Heligmite A stalagmite growing away from the vertical and often changing the direction of its growth.

Hydrology The scientific study of water and water passages underground.

Hypogean The zones below the endogean (or surface) zones.

Ice Age The last period when Britain was covered with ice.

Ice cave A cave, usually at high altitude, which has permanent icicles and frozen floor.

Interstices Small spaces or cracks in the rock.

Joint The natural division of rock, other than a bedding plane, usually at right angles to it. A joint may be confined to one bed or traverse several beds when it is known as a master joint.

Karabiner A metal snap ring, in various shapes with locking devices, for fastening to ropes, linking ladders, using on belays.

Karst or karstland Usually any limestone region which is dry and barren on the surface and is drained by underground channels, the geology of which is specially suitable for the creation of caves, potholes and sinkholes. Derived from the region of the Dinaric 'Alps along the east coast of the Adriatic between Yugoslavia, Albania and Italy.

Knee wrecker Any crawl with accretions on the floor painful to traverse unless the knees are protected with pads.

Labyrinth A maze or complex of cave passages.

Landslip cavern Cave revealed or created by the downward movement of a mountain mass.

Lava cave Cave found in laval fields surrounding extinct volcanoes, sometimes known as Pahoehoe Pots after the Hawaiian term for 'ropy' or 'corded' lava.

Ledgements Wooden platforms in mine workings.

Lench A landing place in a mine.

Letterbox A variation on a cat hole; a narrow slit in the rock.

Level A horizontal gallery in a mine.

Lifeline The safety rope attached to a caver negotiating a pitch to safeguard against a fall or to assist in the ascent.

Limestone The general term given for the bedded rock composed essentially of calcium carbonate, soluble in weak solutions of carbon dioxide and sulphur dioxide in rain water.

Littoral cave A cave found in rocks at the edge of the sea or lake frequently caused by wave action expanding a natural fissure.

Loess Dust or silt deposit, usually rich in lime, occurring in some parts of the world, mainly in northern China where it has been dug out to make cave dwellings.

Master cave The main passage in a system into which all other passages eventually converge.

Maypole A scaling pole, often jointed, to reach higher passages.

Maze A complicated system of passages in which entrances and exits are difficult to find.

Meander A winding cleft or passage in a cave.

Moon (or mountain) milk Calcite in a creamy, liquid form or like cheese which has not set.

Network A cave system of related and intersection passages.

Ogof Welsh word for a cave.

Oolith Ellipsoidal or spherical bodies composed of concentric layers of calcite, aragonite or iron carbonate. Small cave pearls.

Ooze A deposit of calcareous and siliceous skeletons of sea organisms.

Oxbow A loop passage which formerly contained water.

Padding Protective cloth or other suitable material to prevent abrasion of ropes used in SRT.

Percolation Water seepage from the surface.

Permeability The ability of water to pass through pores in the rock, joints and bedding planes.

pH value A convenient method of expressing differences in acidity or alkilinity of a solution in factors between 0 and 14, and is a measure of the hydrogen-ion content. A pH value of 7 is the neutral point. Values above 7 are alkaline; below 7 are acid.

Phreatic zone Waterlogged zone in an area of permeable rock.

Pisolith See **Cave pearl**.

Pitch A vertical section of a cave which requires laddering. Cave guide books give the measurements in feet of the different pitches, the amount of ladder and lifeline required.

Piton A metal peg used as a means of securing a ladder; providing a belaying point.

Pothole Generally, any vertical shaft. It can be a direct entrance into the limestone, or it may be found in a cave.

Prusik Originally a technique of climbing back up a rope, to escape from a crevasse by use of a friction hitch from a subsidiary rope providing footloops on the main rope. Now the general name given to the various metal clamps which grasp the rope in order to ascend; also called ascenders.

Reptation A word used by French cavers to indicate travelling like a reptile in a confined space, sometimes proceeding naked and dragging one's equipment fastened to one's ankle, so as to be able to manoeuvre in the tightest possible space.

Resurgence The emergence of water from an underground stream at the surface.

Rift A fissure with parallel sides between joints and faults.

Rimstone Formation which has grown to form the edge of a pool, deposited by the overflow water (see **Gour**).

Rising A point where water from an underground source rises to the surface.

River cave A cave containing a deep running stream passage for which one requires boats or other forms of floatation to traverse.

Rock milk A soft form of calcite (see **Moon or mountain milk**).

Rock mill   A hole in a stream bed made by stones spun around by the water force.

Rock shelter   A shallow cave entrance, sometimes natural, sometimes man-made to provide a simple abode for a cave dweller.

Ruckle   A mass of jumbled boulders.

Rudaceous deposits   Sometimes known as 'psephites'. Unconsolidated rock fragments of gravel, scree or boulder clay.

Run   A branch of a vein in a Derbyshire lead mine.

Sandstone cave   A cavern in sandstone caused by wind and water action, sometimes by collapse and sometimes by mining.

Saturated   Waterlogged.

Scalenohedral crystal   See **Dog tooth crystal**.

Scallop   See **Current marks**.

Selenite   Crystallised variety of gypsum.

Shaft   The vertical entrance to a mine; also a pitch of a pothole.

Shakehole   A depression of the surface in limestone country indicating the collapse of a cave or a pothole beneath.

Shale   A fine-grained sedimentary rock produced from hardened clay often found in the interstices of limestone.

Sink or sinkhole   A point where water drops underground or has previously done so.

Sinter   See **Travertine**.

Siphon   A passage where water flows by simple siphonic action.

Slickensides   The polish and grooves caused by friction and movement of one rock face against another.

Slocker   A Mendip term for pothole or swallet.

Speleology or spelaeology   The science of cave exploration.

Spelunker   The American name for a speleologist.

Spongework   Raw materials for chert layers in some limestones. A mass of tubular passages, which look like a sponge.

Squeeze   A tight passage through which it is just possible to wriggle one's body.

Stalactite   Formations suspended from the roof of a cave, mainly formed from calcite.

Stalacto-stalagmite   American term for what is often called in Britain a column. Where a stalactite and stalagmite bond together.

Stalagmite   The reverse of a stalactite, i.e. columns of calcite extending upwards from a cave floor.

Stemple   A lead-mining term for wood or metal wedged across a narrow passage in the form of a ladder, or a place for hoisting something.

Straw stalactite   A stalactite, thin-walled and regular in shape like a straw.

Streamway   Stream or river passage through a cave.

Strike   The horizontal line of a bedding plane at right angles to the true dip; the direction along which an ore body runs.

Sump   Point in a cave where water reaches the roof, a water trap, which may be passed only by free-diving, or with equipment, or by baling to create an air space. Often, the limit of exploration.

Swallet   Openings in limestone into which streams disappear underground.

Tail   End of a rope or electron ladder beyond the last run – opposite of a header.

Threshold   Entrance to a cave or pothole to the ultimate limit of natural light.

Trap   See **Sump**.

Traverse   Sometimes used to denote the complete transit of a cave passage or from one system to another; or a horizontal move whilst climbing.

Travertine   Calcium carbonate deposit produced by an underground spring. Most commonly produced in hot springs such as Yellowstone Park, Bath or Buxton.

Troglobite   The biological name for creatures living permanently in the dark or hypogean areas of caves.

Troglodyte   A human cave dweller.

Troglophile   A creature which may live permanently in the dark zone of a cave, but which may also inhabit the endogean areas as well.

Trogloxene   A creature which may enter a cave, e.g. a bat, but does not live there permanently.

Tube   An almost circular cave passage.

Uncomformity   A break in the sequence of rocks in which beds repose on other beds out of precedence in their geological succession.

Vadose zone   The zone above the water table through which water seeps downwards to the zone of saturation.

Water table   The upper limit of a phreatic zone.

Wet suit   An anti-exposure suit made from neoprene designed to keep out cold and wet; made in thicknesses of 4 mm, 5 mm and 6 mm and lined.

BIBLIOGRAPHY

Baker, E.A., *Moors, Crags and Caves of Derbyshire*, John Heywood.

Ballard, Jim, *Spur Book of Caving*.

Barrington, Nicholas, *The Caves of Mendip*, Dalesman Publishing.

Bedford, Bruce, *Challenge Underground*, Allen & Unwin.

Blashford-Snell, John and Richard Snailham. 'Expedition Organising', *Daily Telegraph* 1978.

Bögli & Franke, *Radiant Darkness*, Harrap.

Bristol Speleological Society, *Caves of N.W. Clare*, David & Charles.

British Caving, Routledge & Kegan Paul.

Brook, D.B. and A.C. Waltham, *Caves of Mulu*, Royal Geographical Society.

Cadoux, Jean, *One Thousand Metres Down*, Faber & Faber.

Casteret, Norbert, *Ten Years under the Earth; More Years under the Earth, Cave men old and new;* and *Descent of Pierre St Martin*, J.M. Dent.

'Cave Exploration in Canada', *The Canadian Caver*.

Chevalier, Pierre, *Subterranean Climbers*, Faber & Faber.

Coleman, J.C., *The Caves of Ireland*, Anvil Books.

Cons, David, *Cavecraft*, Harrap.

Courbon, Paul, *Atlas de Grandes Gouffres de Monde*, Jean Lafitte, Marseille.

Elliott, Dave, *Caves of Northern Derbyshire*, Dave Elliott.

Expedition to the Gouffre Berger '67, Pegasus Club, Nottingham.

Ford, Trevor, *The Caves of Derbyshire*, Dalesman Publishing.

Gemmell, Arthur and Meyers, J.O., *Underground Adventure*, Dalesman Publishing.

Grampian Speleological Group, *Appin Cave Guide; The Caves of Assynt*.

Halliday, William R., *Depths of the Earth*, Harper & Row.

Holland, Eric G., *Underground in Furness*, Dalesman Publishing.

Jasinski, Marc, *Caves and Caving*, Paul Hamlyn.

Jenkins, D.W. and Ann Mason Williams, *Wales – Caves in Wales and the Marches*, Dalesman Publishing.

Johnson, Peter, *The History of Mendip Caving*, David & Charles.

Judson, David, *Ghar Parau*, Cassell.

Karst in China, Shanghai People's Publishing House.

Kühn, Herbert, *On Track of Prehistoric Man*, Hutchinson.

Lawrence, Joe Jr., and Roger Brucker, *The Caves Beyond*, Zephyrus Press.

Lovelock, James, *Life and Death Underground*, Bell & Co.

Martel, E.-A., *Irlande et Cavernes Anglaises 1897*. Out of print. *La France Ignorée*, reprinted Laffitte Reprints, Marseille.

Mason, Edmund J., *Caves and Caving in Britain*, Robert Hale.

Mountain Rescue Committee, *Mountain and Cave Rescue*.

Nelson, A. and K.D., *Dictionary of Applied Geology*, Newnes.

Oldham, Tony and Anne, *Discovering Caves*, and *The Caves of Scotland* (except Assynt), Shire Publications.

Pennington, Rooke, *Barrows and Bone Caves of Derbyshire*, Macmillan.

Porteus, Crichton, *Caves and Caverns of Peakland*, Come-to-Derbyshire Association.

Siffre, Marcel, *Beyond Time*, Chatto & Windus.

Tazieff, Haroun, *Caves of Adventure*, Hamish Hamilton.

Thornber, Norman, *Pennine Underground*, Dalesman Publishing.

Ucko and Rosenfeld, *Paleolithic Cave Art*, World Scientific Library.

Waltham, A.C., *Caves*, Macmillan. *The world of Caves*, Orbis Publishing.

Yorkshire Dales – Northern Caves, Vols I to V, Dalesman Publishing.

Diving

Boon, Mike, *Down to a Sunless Sea*, Stalactite Press, Edmonton.

British Sub-Aqua Club Diving Manual.

Burgess, Robert F., *The Cave Divers*, Dodd, Mead & Co., New York.

Farr, Martyn, *The Darkness Beckons*, Diadem Books.

de Lavaur, Guy, *Caves and Cave Diving*, Scientific Book Club.

Lloyd, Oliver C., *Cave Diver's Training Manual*, Cave Diving Group.

Single Rope Techniques

Meredith, Mike, 'Vertical Caving', *Westmoreland Gazette*.

Montgomery, Neil, *Single Rope Techniques*, Sydney Speleological Society.

Thrun, Robert, *Prusiking*, National Speleological Society, Alabama.

Surveying

Ellis, Bryan, *Surveying Caves*, British Cave Research Association.

Periodicals

The British Caver (Editor Tony Oldham), Rhychydwr, Crymych, Dyfed.

Caves and Caving (BCRA) (Editor C.J. Travis), obtainable from B.M. Ellis, 30 Main Road, Westonzoyland, Bridgwater, Somerset.

Caving International (Editor Peter Thomspon), PO Box 4328, Edmonton, Alberta T6E 4T3, Canada.

Descent (Editor Bruce L. Bedford), Mendip Publishing, 30 Drake Road, Wells, Somerset.

Diver (Editor Bernard Eaton), 40 Grays Inn Road, London WC1X 8LR.

INDEX

Holland, *Caves of*, 131, 132

Ilam Risings, 73
India, *Caves of*, 132
Iran, 23
Ireland, *Caves of*, 102
Italy, *Caves of*, 125

Jackson, Peter, 62
Joly de, Robert, 59
Jones, J.A. (Mining), 28

Keld Head, 23, 68, 69, 70, 71
Kerr, Andrew, 45, 73
Kingsdale Master Cave, 70
Kyndwr Club, 20

Lamb Lair (Leer), 19
Lancaster Hole, 94
Langstrath Cave, 39
Langstrath Pot, 39
Leakey, Bob, 66
Leeds Speleological Society, 38
Leger, Bertrand, 71
Le Prieur Commander, 67
Letrone, Michel, 73
Link Pot, 94
Little, Bill, 77
Lloyd, John, 15
Lloyd, Oliver C., 73
Lord's Tot Hole, 80
Loubens, Marcel, 46
Lyon, 'Ben', 29

Mackin, Bob, 70
Marriott, James Gordon, 71
Martel, Edouard-Alfred, 16, 17, 18, 19, 24
Marvel, PC Richard, 64
Maskhill Mine, 45
Mendip, *Caves of*, 97
Mendip Hills, 22, 66
Mexico, *Caves of*, 112
Mont Blanc, 16
Montespan Grotto, 65
Moorhouse, Denny, 54
Morris, Dave, 68
Moss, Neil, 26
Mossdale Beck, 38
Mossdale Cave, 39, 75
Murith, Abbé, 16

Neander Valley, 12
Neanderthal Man, 12
Negri, 68
Nelson, Mike, 73
Nent Head, 52
Nettle Pot, 20
Newcastle University CC, 39
New Guinea, 23
New Guinea, *Caves of* (see South-East Asia)
Northern Cave & Fell Club, 66
Norway, 23
Norway, *Caves of*, 125, 126
Nullabur Plain, 71

Ogof Afon Hepste, 73
Ogof Ffynnon Ddu, 38, 64, 68, 77, 94
Oldham Batteries, 28
Ottonelli, 65, 68

Oxclose, 80
Oxlow Mine, 29, 80

Paris, Spéléo Club de, 71
Peak Cavern, 15, 16, 26, 65
Pearce, Dr Ken, 70, 71, 73

Railton, Lewis, 77
Raspo Abyss, 15
Revel, Roland, 25
Rouquayrol & Denarouze, 66

Salmon, Les, 63
Sarawak, 23
Sarawak, *Caves of* (see South-East Asia)
Saussure, de, 16
Scotland, *Caves of*, 104, 105
Sheppard, Jack, 66
Siebe, Gorman & Co., 67
Simpson, E., 24
Single Rope Technique, 42 ff
Société de Spéléologique de France, 20
Solari, Roger, 73
South America, *Caves of*, 112
South-East Asia, *Caves of*, 119
Spain & Portugal, *Caves of*, 127
Speleophone, 70
Spluga della Preta, 46
Staniforth, John, 64
Statham, Oliver, 23, 68, 70, 71
Stockport Odd Feet Association, 30
Stoke Lane Slocker, 62
Swildon's Hole, 19, 64
Switzerland, *Caves of*, 130

Tarbuck, Ken, 48
Tot Lord's Hole, 80
Tratman, Dr Edgar, 22
Trebiciano, Grotto di, 15
Triestine, Casso, 15
Trou du Glaz, 59
Trou Madame, 71

UIAA, 51
USSR, *Caves of*, 120

Vaucluse, Fontaine de, 65, 68
Vidor Batteries, 28
Viking Caving Club, 70
Von Vavasour, 12

Wales, *Caves of*, 101
Waltham, Dr Antony, 22
Walton, Isaak, 12
Weill's disease, 62
Wells, Natural History Society, 20
West Wycombe caves, 105
Whernside Manor caving centre, 29, 32
Whillans, Don, 56
White Rose Club, 64
Wookey Hole, 19, 67, 68, 71
Workman, Geoff, 19

Yeadon, Geoff, 23, 69, 70, 71
Yorkshire, 22
Yorkshire, *Caves of*, 101
Yorkshire Ramblers' Club, 19, 20

Zagros mountains, 29